D0597786

Spas

Exceptional Destinations Around the World

Eloise Napier

Spas

Exceptional Destinations Around the World

Abbeville Press Publishers

New York   London

For my father

Many thanks to Charlotte Eager, Janet Goldby
Frances Power, Sarah Barclay, Annabel Meggeson,
Toby Mansel-Pleydell and Henrietta Creighton
for all their help.

Front jacket photograph: Ari Magg (model: Anna Rakel/
Eskimo models), Blue Lagoon, Iceland. Back jacket
photograph: Jan Kassay/Sanctuary Zara Spa

First published in the United States of America
in 2003 by Abbeville Press, 116 West 23rd Street,
New York, N.Y. 10011

First published in Great Britain in 2002 by
Conran Octopus Limited, a part of the Octopus
Publishing Group, 2-4 Heron Quays,
London E14 4JP

Library of Congress Control Number TK

First edition

10 9 8 7 6 5 4 3 2 1

ISBN: 0-7892-0798-2

Publishing Director: Lorraine Dickey
Senior Editor Katey Day
Creative Director: Leslie Harrington
Designer: Jeremy Tilston
Picture Research: Sian Lloyd
Production Director: Julie Young
Senior Production Controller: Manjit Sihra

Contents

A Place to Spa

Relief. That is the essence of a spa — relief from the pressures of everyday life, from the aches and pains of a tired body, from the anxieties of an overworked brain.

Everyone has his or her own method of winding down — whether it's by lying on a beach being plied with alcohol and regular massages, undergoing an ancient cleansing ritual, sitting under a waterfall in the middle of a rainforest, or taking vigorous exercise tempered with spiritual pursuits such as meditation or t'ai chi. You may wish to go alone or with a lover or even with an entire family. Sometimes you may have only a day to indulge yourself. Or, if you are incredibly lucky, you might be able to spend as long as six weeks.

Finding a spa that provides the ideal combination of qualities to suit your needs — which can change from month to month — is more complicated than it first appears. There are so many choices to make and so many locations to choose from that you can end up buried in too much information. As a result, finding the perfect destination becomes so difficult that you feel dazed and confused and in more need of a rest than ever.

Spas: Exceptional Destinations Around the World focuses on 25 of the world's most exceptional destination spas. Each one provides a memorable experience and offers, to varying degrees, a combination of indulgence, adventure, health and relaxation. Some of these spas will change your life for good, others will rejuvenate you in the short term so that you can return to your normal life feeling refreshed and reenergized.

A trip to a destination spa should be an adventure. Its location, blended with the excellence of its therapies and quality of service, should make it an outstanding place to visit. The journey to reach some of these far-flung spots can be an adventure in itself. This, though, is all part of the fun.

And a spa, as much as anything else, should be fun. Try as you might, it is hard to escape the absurdity factor inherent in many treatments — being wrapped from head to foot in mud and then encased in large sheets of plastic wrap may be an effective way of extracting toxins, but it is virtually impossible to keep a straight face at the same time. Lying on a bed being prodded by hot and cold stones sounds like a fairly ridiculous pastime, yet the resultant physical and emotional relief that it provides can be miraculous.

Spas: Exceptional Destinations Around the World covers the full gamut of destination resorts. There are mind/body retreats where yoga, meditation and gentle massage help you to regain your equilibrium and find inner peace. There are luxurious spas where indulgence and pampering are key, and health farms specializing in treatments to help you lose weight and formulate new healthy living patterns. For adrenaline junkies there are activity breaks on which you can exercise and tone your body into a different shape. Finally, there are the eco-retreats where you can simply surrender yourself to the healing power of nature.

Spa treatments will probably take up only a few hours of each day. To stave off the possibility of boredom, each one of the spas featured offers you the opportunity to pursue umpteen activities including golf, skiing, diving, deep-sea fishing, sightseeing, hiking, bird watching and horseback riding. Some spas welcome children with open arms and have separate facilities so that offspring are entertained (and usually exhausted) while parents retreat to a different area to relax and be pampered in unaccustomed peace. Other resorts are only for adults and are perfect for romantic breaks or for those who seek solace in solitude.

Whatever type of spa you choose to visit there is one key thing to remember: this is your time for healing. There is no right way or wrong way, just one that suits you best.

Agua at the Delano, South Beach, Miami, USA

ABOVE: THE RECEPTION AREA AT THE DELANO

In some ways it seems a shame to describe the Delano — the less you know about it beforehand, the better the surprise, yet even a description will not fully prepare you for what to expect.

Walking through the door is like stepping into a scene from *Alice in Wonderland* — the lobby is enormous, full of huge, eclectic pieces of furniture, including a surrealist Salvador Dali chair and a fur-covered ottoman. There are massive columns, dark paneled walls and a series of billowing white curtains. People are scattered all around the lobby, some drinking cocktails, others smoking cigars; everyone is beautiful and they are all watching each other. This is "hotel as theater" at its very best, and beyond your wildest dreams.

The Delano is a joint creation of the international hotelier Ian Schrager and the French designer Philippe Starck. They have produced what Schrager describes as an "urban resort" where people can escape from Miami, one of the most exuberant cities in the world, into a cool haven of peace. And it is cool — in every sense of the word. The Delano is frequented by the celebrity A-list — Harrison Ford, George Clooney, Donatella Versace and Calvin Klein — to name just the tips of the iceberg.

A red-paneled elevator moves from the spectacle that is the lobby to the penthouse, which houses Agua — a serene retreat within a retreat. This über-chic designer spa was created by Schrager's wife, Rita, and Leila Fazel. Everything about the design is clever, but very, very simple. Everything is white, from the staff's uniforms to the floating curtains that separate the treatment areas. It is so perfect that, now and then, Madonna wanders in and books the entire place.

ABOVE: THE SAUNA   ABOVE: THE SECLUDED ROOF TERRACE

Agua at the Delano is ideal for women who want a sanctuary of peace in an otherwise hectic day. Time seems to slow when you enter its doors — the mood is very intimate and very peaceful and everyone speaks in whispers. Its philosophy is simple: less is more. As Rita Schrager puts it: "We didn't want people to feel rushed, even if they were coming for half an hour; we didn't want exotic names for the treatments — we wanted things that gave instant results or made you feel better."

Leila Fazel continues: "Agua is designed to take you out of yourself — you are no longer in the Delano. You don't know where you are, you are just floating."

They have been so successful that even the background music fades into nothing more than white noise. Agua is very glamorous in its simplicity, but it is not intimidating. The lack of walls, which can be slightly unnerving at first, fosters a feeling of community. Men are not allowed in until the evenings, so if you want to sunbathe nude on the rooftop terrace, known as the Solarium, there is nothing to stop you. The treatments, ranging from Eve Lom facials through to Biologique Recherche manual-lift facial sessions (with or without oxygen), cater to the professional beauty addict. There is also what is referred to as a "back facial" — an hour of deep-pore cleansing for the upper back that includes a hydrating mask.

The spa's signature treatment – the Ayurvedic milk-and-honey massage – is not to be missed. An invigorating rub down is followed by a massage with a mixture of honey and organic sesame seed oil, which is then cleansed away with buttermilk. Suddenly, you know what Cleopatra felt like.

The treatments do not have to take place in the Agua –a selection of massages (including cranio-sacral, deep tissue, shiatsu and pregnancy) are available in either the orchard or an Arabian tent on the beach. You can doze by the pool – known as the Water Salon – and have a reflexology session at the same time. But best of all, Agua offers 24-hour room service. After a mad party you can treat yourself to an hour of aromatherapy massage at three o'clock in the morning. Or, if you feel so inclined, visit the state-of-the-art gym – also open around the clock.

ABOVE: THE FAMOUS DELANO SWIMMING POOL WITH TABLE AND CHAIRS IN THE SHALLOW END

"We're not trying to be tasteful — others out there can do that. This is a separate reality — you're not just checking into a hotel room and going to sleep." With a life-size chess set placed in the garden below the Delano, Ian Schrager has a point. Even the bedrooms in the hotel feel like a film set. They are white, very white. Philippe Starck claims that the color scheme runs from white to pearl gray, but the gradation is imperceptible. Virtually the only color comes from a fresh green apple placed on a metal plinth by the door, with a note underneath that reads, "An apple a day keeps the doctor away."

The rooms may be quirky, but the attention to detail is second to none. Blankets, handwoven in India exclusively for the Delano, are draped over each bed. In some of the larger suites and in the poolside bungalows there are plasma flat-screen televisions with automatic five-disc DVD changers. The bathrooms offer complimentary aromatherapy gels and salts, natural sea sponges, votive candles and lavender potpourri from Provence.

Just down from the Water Salon, with its elegant table and chairs in the shallow end, lies the Delano's Beach Village, which comprises a series of tents and cabanas, the centerpiece of which is a 12-meter (40-foot) pastel-striped tented lighthouse. It is all delightfully and gloriously eccentric — but very comfortable. Food and drinks are served from the Beach Grill and Barbecue, and you can run from the sea straight on to a massage table, have a t'ai chi lesson or play a game of beach volleyball.

ABOVE: MIAMI BEACH

Food at the Delano is also served at the Blue Door restaurant (where, of course, there is no door, blue or otherwise). The cuisine is imaginative: foie-gras burgers (duck liver with caramelized onion and ketchup on a small bun), blue crab with guacamole, and jumbo shrimps with tempura leeks and pomegranate sauce. Positioned next to the Blue Door is the Brasserie — very "Harry's Bar-in-Venice" in style. Although the food here is as good as any you will find in Miami, few people come here just to eat. Looking, as it does, straight on to the lobby, the Blue Door is the city's ultimate spot for people watching.

The Delano is self-awareness encapsulated — but then that is its raison d'être. And if it all gets a bit much, you can always withdraw to the gentle comfort zone that is the Agua.

AGUA
DELANO HOTEL
1685 COLLINS AVENUE
MIAMI BEACH, FLORIDA 33139
TEL: 305 672 2000
FAX: 305 532 0099
DELANO@IANSCHRAGERHOTELS.COM
WWW.IANSCHRAGERHOTELS.COM

Agua at the Delano, South Beach, Miami, USA   15

Young children have a knack of leaving their parents gasping with exhaustion. Finding a place to be spoiled in comfort, knowing that those offspring are being safely entertained, is like striking gold. To do this somewhere that is achingly hip sounds nearly impossible.

Babington House achieves all of this and much, much more. Set in the rolling countryside of Somerset, this elegant Georgian building is owned by the highly fashionable London members' club Soho House, which transformed it from a family home into a hotel and spa in 1998. None of the country house feel has been lost — all the communal rooms are scattered with newspapers and have roaring log fires and comfy sofas — yet there is not a hint of chintz anywhere. Unsurprisingly, given the strong metropolitan connection, interior design is an important factor here.

The impression of staying at a grand country home is reinforced by the manicured grounds that surround the house. Beyond the croquet lawn there is a small reed-framed lake, and next door to that is a cricket pitch and a five-a-side soccer field. Humor is never very far away and the old livestock barn, today known as the Cowshed, has been imaginatively turned into a spa with indoor and outdoor heated swimming pools, sauna, steam room and various treatment areas. More treatments take place in a recent, charmingly quirky addition: a yurt in the garden. Close enough for reassurance, but out of earshot, is the childcare facility.

Babington is so relaxed that anything goes. Indulgence is key — having a massage and a facial swiftly followed by an entire tub of Ben and Jerry's ice cream will not raise an eyebrow.

ABOVE: THE BAR

Babington House, Somerset, UK

Because most guests usually stay for short breaks, the treatments in the Cowshed concentrate more on beauty and relaxation than anything else. There are, of course, detoxifying routines, and the aromatherapy salt rubs followed by holistic massage or a mineral-rich algae wrap are out of this world. An assortment of different massages are also available, from Indian head massage, Thai and sports massages to reflexology and what is referred to as "Stoned Cow" — a Native American full-body massage using smooth hot and cold stones.

Admirably energetic and fully qualified caregivers are on hand to look after children in the childcare facility throughout the day; hence the spa is very popular with young mothers hoping for a combination of respite and pampering. One of the most frequently requested therapies is the hydrotherm massage, which is particularly suitable for pregnant women. This involves lying supine on a large, warm water-filled bag that supports the body while a head-to-toe massage soothes tensions away.

The Cowshed produces a range of extremely effective skincare and bath products, which were originally created for use only in the spa and the hotel but are now sold worldwide. Each preparation is carefully made by hand using essential aromatherapy oils and botanical extracts. The herbal infusions are astrologically sourced from the estate's walled organic kitchen garden, which guests are encouraged to wander in and which supplies many of the ingredients used in the Cowshed's juice bar. The names of the products are delightfully eccentric and guaranteed to raise a smile: the face creams are called "Cheeky Cow"; the aphrodisiac bath oil, "Horny Cow," is highly recommended; and the "Grumpy Cow" morning shower gel is a brilliantly effective pick-me-up.

ABOVE: THE INDOOR SWIMMING POOL — ONCE POPULATED BY A HERD OF COWS

The spa is continually changing, with new products and treatments being developed all the time. Many of the latest skincare lotions are so dependent upon fresh ingredients, such as yogurt, honey, herbs, fruit, flowers and oats, that they can only be used on site. Alarmingly, not only do they smell fabulous, they generally taste pretty good, too. Massages and facials in the new yurt are sublime — there can be snow on the ground outside and yet inside it will be deliciously warm and peaceful, with only the gentle quacking of the ducks on the lake to disturb you.

The bedrooms at Babington are totally different from one another, but each is so sensuous that it is tempting never to emerge. The design is contemporary and simple, with generous use of natural materials. The beds are vast, with masses of crisp white pillows. One bedroom has an open-air tub big enough for two, with views of undulating hills and hedgerows that stretch for miles. Others have elegant free-standing baths in the middle of the room, while each has a selection of complimentary industrial-sized bottles filled with Cowshed lotions and potions. Leather sofas, flat-screen televisions, DVD players, internet access and digital television combine to make these rooms utterly luxurious.

RIGHT: THE HISTORIC CITY OF BATH LIES A SHORT DRIVE AWAY

The accommodation is split into four areas: the main house, the Coach House, the Stable Rooms and the Lodge (a three-bedroom self-contained house at the entrance to the property that is rented out for a week at a time.) The Coach House and the Stable Rooms are a two-minute walk away from the main house. The Stables have been converted into family-size studio flats with two bedrooms, one endowed with bunk beds, a shower room and a bath the size of a small pond. If you are seeking peace and quiet, do not be put off by the fact that children are so welcome — Babington is extraordinarily well organized and has so much space that you very rarely notice there are little ones around.

Entertainment is taken very seriously. There is a state-of-the-art cinema, seating up to 45 people, which regularly shows current films and pre-release screenings. If you can't make it that far, there is a library of DVD films that can be watched in your bedroom. The bar and the billiard room are comfortably distracting, but for a spot of energetic activity there is a brand-new gym and a schedule of exercise classes that includes boxercise, yoga and circuit training.

The cuisine, which leans toward Italy and the Mediterranean for its inspiration, is as good as anything you will find in the heart of London. Breakfast, however, is resoundingly British and triumphantly hearty, with enormous quantities of coffee, tea, thick buttered toast with marmalade or Marmite and a buffet groaning with homemade cereals, muffins, croissants and fruit juice. The bacon rolls and eggs Benedict are famous specialities.

Babington House's rare combination of virtues means that it is one of the very few places where a diverse mixture of people — funky media types, romantic couples, pregnant women and toddlers — can all thoroughly enjoy themselves (and one another) without feeling remotely self-conscious. This, above all, is what makes staying there such fun.

BABINGTON HOUSE
BABINGTON
FROME
SOMERSET BA 11 3RW UK
TEL: +44 1373 812 266
FAX: +44 1373 812 112
BABHOUSE@COMPUSERVE.COM
WWW.BABINGTONHOUSE.CO.UK

Blue Lagoon,
Grindavík, Iceland

Imagine living in a place that looks like a lunar landscape, where a considerable percentage of your social life is spent throat-deep in a hot pond and the greatest natural landmark of the area happens to be right next door to a huge, smoking power station. It sounds bizarre, but that's Iceland for you.

The Blue Lagoon is a vast, steaming geothermal seawater pool. Situated halfway between the country's capital, Reykjavík, and the main airport, it is a popular place for travelers who want to bask in its aquamarine waters and reap the benefits of the mineralized mud.

Iceland lies on a spot where two tectonic plates meet — hence the dramatic treeless lava landscape. This is also why the area is awash with geothermal water: local people have occasionally found hot springs bubbling up into their living rooms thanks to the constant activity going on under the Earth's crust. However, the Icelanders have become adept at harnessing nature's powerful forces. Geothermal seawater is extracted from underground lakes at 160°C (320°F) and then is used to heat springwater for part of Iceland's central heating. When the seawater is released from the power station it is cooled in special wells before flowing into the lava field that, over the years, has become the Blue Lagoon.

The seawater in the lagoon is clean and unpolluted. With its temperature of 36-39°C (96-102°F) and salt concentration equivalent to the sea, it has developed its own eco-system with high levels of silica, minerals and algae. The latter account for the startling blueness of the water, while the silica mud is ideal for exfoliating the body and the minerals are said to heal skin disorders, certain forms of arthritis and even asthma.

Blue Lagoon, Grindavík, Iceland

It is freezing cold, there is snow on the ground and the lifeguards are all wearing goosedown jackets, gloves and thick hats. You, meanwhile, are clad in a swimming costume and sitting in an enormous hot pool, wondering why the appalling smell of sulphur that assaulted you on arrival miraculously seems no longer to matter. The steam, which rises like a mist off the lagoon, obscures those around you so that they appear surreal, like ghostly figures. Whatever worries you may have brought with you dissolve under the impact of this primordial setting.

When workers from the nearby power station found that bathing in the waters of the lagoon improved chronic skin complaints, word soon spread and in 1994 the Clinic for Natural Treatment of Psoriasis opened on its banks. Officially backed by the Icelandic government, the clinic offers specialist treatment, personalized to suit each patient. To gain the maximum benefit, a three- to four-week stay is recommended

Although locals, from businessmen through housewives and their children, use the pools several times a week — they function like an open-air village hall — most foreign visitors tend to drop in for a couple of hours, or a day at the most. As the area has grown more popular, the facilities have improved. Where once there was just a pond and a reception shed, there is now a full-blown spa where you can hire bathing costumes, towels and robes, buy items from the Blue Lagoon skincare range and have a full-body aromatherapy massage in one of the lava pools. Lava caves now play host to an indoor geothermal steam-bath and waist-height pool.

The spa packages are relatively simple and involve either a full-body or shoulder massage with essential oils, followed by a silica mud mask. There is nothing, however, to stop you from applying an all-over do-it-yourself mud pack — just bend down and pick up handfuls of the gloop, then smear it across yourself. You'll feel like a child indulging in body painting and there is something wonderfully therapeutic, both mentally and physically, about it. If the smell of the water becomes overwhelming, you can move to the adjacent geothermal beach and watch everyone else wallowing like ancient painted tribal warriors.

TOP RIGHT: THE RESTAURANT WITH ITS PANORAMIC VIEWS OVER THE LAGOON

MIDDLE RIGHT: APPLYING A DO-IT-YOURSELF MUD PACK

BOTTOM RIGHT: NEW BRIDGES AND WALKWAYS MAKE ACCESS TO THE BLUE LAGOON EASIER THAN EVER

Blue Lagoon, Grindavík, Iceland

When you have had enough of the steam, water and mud, the spa complex includes a gourmet restaurant, conference center, cafeteria and gift shop. There is an extremely good set of changing rooms, which is essential because after a session in the lagoon you come out with hair that feels like straw. The food is fine but there are some unusual combinations – beetroot and pickled herring sandwiches are definitely an acquired taste.

For those attending the clinic and, as a result, remaining in the area for some length of time, the Blue Lagoon Hotel is the closest place to stay. Offering family-style hospitality it has 21 rooms, each equipped with satellite television, geothermal showers and mini-bars. There is also an in-house Jacuzzi and sauna, although with so much water and steam outside, they may seem a little superfluous.

Most day-trip visitors to the Blue Lagoon stay in Reykjavík. Iceland's capital is one of the funkiest cities in the world and enormous fun. There are countless hotels to stay at but both the Hotel Saga and the Hotel Esja are comfortable and have creditable spas where you can indulge in any number of wraps, massages, scrubs, pedicures, manicures and facials.

The time of year when you visit the Blue Lagoon is immaterial– it is never less than staggeringly impressive. In the winter months you have the chance to witness the ethereal dance of the Northern lights; in the summer the nights glow with midnight sunsets. There are innumerable outdoor activities to pursue including some of the best fishing in the world. The terrain is fascinating in its peculiarity, combining immense moss-covered lava fields, steaming craters, spouting geysers and massive glaciers. Many of these can be toured on mountain bikes or on horseback. Hiking holidays are particularly popular, and with so many natural pools available you may well find yourself leaping in and out of them with increasing regularity. There is something strangely comforting about these natural spas and it does not take long to appreciate why Icelanders are so addicted to them.

ABOVE: ICELAND'S CAPITAL, REYKJAVÍK

BLUE LAGOON
SVARTSENGI
P.O. BOX 22
240 GRINDAVIK, ICELAND
TEL: +354 420 8800
FAX: +354 420 8801
WWW.BLUELAGOON.IS

Blue Lagoon, Grindavik, Iceland   27

Canyon Ranch,
Tucson, Arizona, USA

At the foot of the Santa Catalina Mountains, surrounded by cacti, bougainvillaea and dry pebble rivers, lies one of the United States' most renowned health resorts. Once a dude ranch, home to cowboys and herds of cattle, this gem in the desert landscape has been turned into a 70-acre oasis dedicated entirely to well-being.

Opened in 1979, Canyon Ranch is health and fitness on a grand scale: the spa facilities alone (which include seven gyms, specialty weight-training rooms, a meditation dome and three swimming pools) take up 5,600 square meters (64,000 square feet). There are more than 720 staff at Canyon Ranch — three to each guest. The very latest

Western medical practices are combined with a vast array of Eastern and alternative therapies to provide an approach to health that is truly holistic.

The choice of treatments available is mind boggling; with more than 50 exercise and lecture classes to choose from each day it is not surprising that, at the start of each stay, guests are assigned a program coordinator to discuss their aims and decide what will suit them. However, be warned, it is impossible to "do" the Ranch in one visit — to fit everything in you would have to be on the go for 24 hours a day, every day. This helps to explain why 80 percent of guests come back again . . . and again.

Canyon Ranch is fun, but it is also serious. The overriding aim is to help guests to improve their quality of life — both mentally and physically — for good. The Life Enhancement Center is a pivotal part of the resort. It offers popular week-long programs throughout the year, focusing on different aspects of successful aging, from dealing with stress, sexuality and arthritis to heart disease, diabetes and cancer. In this world stethoscopes are as important as Stairmasters.

At Canyon Ranch the key to good health and longevity lies in a combination of exercise, sensible eating, peaceful sleep, serenity of mind and optimism. To this end behavioral therapists and clinical psychologists are on hand to deal with psychological problems, sleep disorders and addictions. Acupuncturists and Chinese herbalists offer alternative solutions that complement the mainstream medicine.

The resort is justifiably proud of its sports facilities. There are more than 25 fitness instructors, along with a chiropractor, five neuromuscular therapists and six physiologists. If they can't sort out a muscular and skeletal problem, it is unlikely that anyone can. There are endless group classes from line dancing and funk aerobics through boxercise and aqua aerobics. The spinning class, a simulated electronic cycle ride through the countryside, is famously exhausting, but effective.

Although we breathe instinctively, few of us breathe properly, which can lead to a buildup of stress levels and a decrease in energy, so the breathing and relaxation classes are well worth attending. These are further enhanced by the daily qi gong, t'ai chi, meditation, Pilates and yoga sessions. Yoga classes range from an introduction to the sun salutation for beginners to 90 minutes of power yoga for those who are more experienced.

Serious walkers will be in their element, and once a year a special hiking week is organized. You have to be fit enough to cover 17–28 kilometers (11–18 miles) a day, and climb 1,200 meters (4,000 feet) over some fairly rocky terrain. However, the canyons and peaks of the Santa Catalina, Rincon and Tucson Mountains are spectacular and it is reassuring to know that any aches, pains or strains can be massaged away back at the ranch.

"It's not the years
you add to your
life, but the life
you add to
your years."

CANYON RANCH PHILOSOPHY

Usually, however, mornings can start with
a gentle hike — or a ski-trek — among the
saguaro cactus and mesquite in the Sonoran
Desert. For those who want to venture
further, there are mountain bikes for rent.
If you are still feeling bouncy — which,
given all the other treatments and the
healthy diet, is likely — squash or tennis
lessons are available from one of the team
of instructors. They are very good, as well
as very tactful — particularly if you need to
reconstruct both your forehand and your
backhand strokes.

Canyon Ranch, Tucson, USA   31

Most people visit to rejuvenate themselves at Canyon Ranch for four to seven days. There are a few strict rules that everyone has to abide by: no alcohol, no smoking indoors and no cell phones other than in the bedrooms. This is not a place for young families. Children have to be at least 14 years old and no one under the age of 18 is allowed to attend the Life Enhancement Center — although, given the nature of the courses (Optimal Aging, Journey through Midlife, A Women's Retreat), they probably would not want to anyway.

Even the pampering treatments are overtly health-conscious — all the massage and body therapies are seen as important factors contributing to the intricate balance of physical, emotional and spiritual well-being, and they are all excellent. The Healing Touch treatment is especially affecting: a nurse dangles metal weights above the body's chakras to discover the state of the body's energy flow and balance, and then kneads away any blockages. One of the unexpected benefits is the emotional release that it can trigger.

Another therapy definitely worth trying is the watsu, which is best described as an aquatic shiatsu. While immersed in a small, body-temperature pool in a large dome decorated with Native American Hopi drawings, the therapist floats and dances your body through the water. It is so relaxing that it is not unusual to fall asleep in the therapist's arms, and any muscular pain seems to dissolve completely.

There is a comprehensive range of skincare and beauty treatments, including hair extensions and even lessons on how to apply sports makeup, although, given the multiplicity of activities to try every day, it would be amazing if anyone had the time or inclination to put on any makeup.

The food at Canyon Ranch is, predictably, very healthy. But it is not just celery stalks and cabbage. The frequently changed menu features kataifi-wrapped lobster tail, sushi, Cantonese tempeh stir-fry, pepper steak and banana crème brûlée, among many other delights. There is fruit everywhere, strategically placed throughout the complex, and the menus list calorie counts and cholesterol figures instead of prices. To ensure the dietary benefits last after you return home, there are various workshops in the demonstration kitchen at which you can learn how to prepare the food you have just eaten.

Everyone stays in one of the 170 casitas, which are perfectly comfortable and functional, if a little bland. However, by the end of the day, all you want is a cozy bed to collapse in before you kick off again at dawn the next morning.

CANYON RANCH
8600 E. ROCKCLIFF ROAD
TUCSON, ARIZONA 85750
TEL: 520 749 9000
FAX: 520 749 7755
WWW.CANYONRANCH.COM

Chiva-Som,
Hua Hin, Thailand

More gain, less pain. Chiva-Som is one of the few places in the world that manages to make the unappealing processes of detoxing and losing weight seem rather enjoyable. The purpose-built health retreat, with its palm trees and verdant gardens, overlooks the Gulf of Thailand, a few minutes walk away from the town of Hua Hin.

Translated, Chiva-Som means Haven of Life and it is indeed an oasis of pampering where relaxation is nothing less than an art form. After the journey there, however, most people definitely need it. The three-hour coach trip from Bangkok airport is beautiful in parts, but the general standard of Thai driving is enough to send your heart into your mouth for most of the way. The Chiva-Som mini-bus driver is perfectly safe — but everyone else seems completely demented. After the chaos on the roads, it is a blissful relief to step into the tranquil atmosphere of the resort, where you are immediately handed a glass of chilled lemongrass water to help you recuperate.

With a staff-to-guest ratio of four to one, you can hardly drop a book without it being recovered for you immediately, and every guest is made to feel immensely special.

Whether you are staying at Chiva-Som for a weekend or a month, the standard fee automatically includes all your meals and a daily massage — Thai, Swedish or G5 Vibro. Apart from the bathing pavilion with its indoor swimming pool, multilevel steam room and Kniepp therapy foot bath, most of the health and beauty treatments cost extra.

Chiva-Som, Hua Hin, Thailand 35

One of the first things you receive on arrival at Chiva-Som is a planning calendar to help you organize all your treatments and activities. It seems an odd notion to have to schedule relaxation, but when you see how many different things are available it begins to make sense. The ambience is very laid back — you can be as active or as lazy as you want to be.

During your initial medical consultation (there is one when you arrive and one when you leave), a nurse asks you about your objectives. "Weight loss, fitness, relaxation and stress reduction, or a general boost to your health?" Probably all of them will apply, but for practicality you will generally focus on just one or two.

As this is Thailand it is almost de rigueur to try one of the legendary Thai massages. Before it starts you are given the option of "gentle, medium or hard" massage, and although you will no doubt be twisted into positions you might assume to be physically impossible, it is far from painful. You can have your session outside or in one of the treatment rooms.

The perfect way to relax after a massage is to have a Bath of Chiva. Tottering back to your room, you will find that your bathtub has been filled to the brim with warm cows' milk, a liberal sprinkling of rose petals floating on the top. Immersing yourself in this scented goo is one of the most sybaritic experiences imaginable. It is also said to be good for the skin, but, frankly, this is of secondary importance – it's much more fun being able to go home and say. "I've bathed in milk from head to toe!" You cannot help but laugh at yourself, and that in itself is relaxing.

For those who need more serious therapy there is a range of medical treatments. These include equilibropathy, which is a unique form of acupuncture focusing on the muscles of the back to improve energy flow and lymphatic drainage. Chi Nei Tsang is an internal-organ massage (performed from the outside) and is particularly effective for dissolving stress, tension and negative emotions. It can be quite painful, however. Iridology, reiki, allergy testing and life coaching are also available.

BELOW: THE POWER SHOWER

BELOW: THE FLOTATION CHAMBER

ABOVE: GUESTS ARE HOUSED IN THE TRADITIONAL THAI-STYLE VILLAS

Virtually everything at Chiva-Som is designed to educate in some way. It is not aggressive, but the therapists will give you advice during your treatments so that you can eliminate damaging aspects of your everyday lifestyle. There are various formal education classes on nutrition, cooking and healing with Bach herbal remedies, along with some more esoteric topics, including aura balancing, hypnotherapy and carved-fruit sculpture.

Day-to-day activities include yoga, Zen meridian stretching (which is great for understanding your body and knowing its limitations), water Pilates, t'ai chi, kick boxing and body sculpting. One of the most uplifting sessions is the early morning mind training that takes place in the yoga pavilion as the sun comes up. An ex-Buddhist monk teaches awareness techniques to help you learn to live in the moment, and not to worry about the past or future. Alternatively, it is extraordinarily calming to visit the beach at this time in the morning when the only people you pass are monks on their way to collect alms.

CHIVA-SOM
73/4 PETCHKASEM ROAD
HUA HIN
PRACHUAB KHIRIKHAM 77110
THAILAND
TEL: +66(0) 3253 6536
FAX: +66(0) 3251 1154
E-MAIL: RESERVATION@CHIVASOM.COM
WWW.CHIVASOM.COM

Much of the food at Chiva-Som is organic and grown on the property, and the ethos is "moderation, not starvation or elimination" according to the head chef, Andrew Jacka. The menus change every six months, but they always have the same key features — little salt, no sugar and minimal fat. Herbs are used imaginatively, and you can expect to eat things such as barley, lime and parsley salad, spiced lentil soup, tofu curry, zucchini pakoras and baked wheat-free apple tart served with cinnamon soy ice cream. The kangaroo fillet is highly recommended. There are also fish and meat alternatives. The menus include calorie, fat and chili ratings. Alcohol, in the form of wine and champagne, is only served after 6 P.M., and although they are discouraged, this applies to cigarettes too. Cell phones are forbidden and guests must be at least 16 years old.

There are 57 bedrooms and suites located in a cluster of traditional Thai-style pavilions in the center of the estate. The rooms are comfortable, if a little small in some cases. The mini-bars are alcohol free and instead are stocked with five different types of mineral water, fruit juice and low-fat coconut health bars.

ABOVE: THE CHIVA-SOM RECEPTION AREA

Chiva-Som claims to judge its success not by what you do while you are there, but rather by what you do when you get home. Do not be surprised if you find yourself buying a juicer.

Clinique La Prairie, Clarens-Montreux, Switzerland

Total reconfiguration seems a lot to expect from a trip to a spa. Yet this is perfectly possible after a visit to Clinique La Prairie, which lies in seclusion on the outskirts of Clarens-Montreux between the Alps and Lac Léman. You can define most spas by genre — thalassotherapy, Ayurvedic, New Age, luxury pampering — but Clinique La Prairie stands out in a class of its own. Part spa, part hospital, part luxury hotel, it is devoted to fighting the effects of aging and to prolonging a healthier life.

This fight takes place on several fronts: the world-class medical clinic specializes in orthopaedic and reconstructive surgery (including pioneering work on prolapsed discs); the dentistry unit can produce a new set of caps within days; while the menopause center concentrates on treatments to combat osteoporosis and fatigue. There is a full range of cosmetic surgery spanning hair grafting, collagen injections, chemical facial peels, liposuction, abdominoplasty and breast augmentation or reduction.

The Clinique has built up an international reputation through a treatment called Cell Therapy in which live fetal sheep cells are injected into the buttocks to accelerate cell activity. The body's rate of cell renewal declines naturally with age, but the injections slow this process and revitalize the immune system — effectively slowing the effects of aging. It sounds bizarre, but the Clinique has pioneered this treatment since 1931 and has a client list that reads like the pages of *Who's Who* — Winston Churchill, Margaret Thatcher, Sylvester Stallone, Cher and Jerry Hall are among many rumored to have benefited from its treatments.

On a more orthodox front, the Clinique runs a series of unique beauty and weight-loss programs that entail massage, exercise, hydrotherapy and detoxification. As the name Beautymed suggests, even the spa treatments are highly scientific.

Clinique La Prairie, Clarens-Montreux, Switzerland   41

All treatments at the Clinique begin with the most thorough medical check-up that you are ever likely to experience at a spa. The programs are normally tailored to last for a week (longer programs are available, but the prices are extreme) and begin on a Sunday, when you are picked up by a chauffeur-driven limousine at Geneva airport. Monday starts with a blood test and blood pressure and weight check before breakfast. The nutritionist will already have visited to work out your diet (there is a popular 1,200-calories-a-day option) and once the medical checks have been done, a breakfast of fruit, muesli, rolls and yogurt is brought to your room.

After this the serious examinations start. A doctor performs exhaustive tests, including an electro-cardiogram and a close scrutiny of every inch of your skin for growths and blemishes. You then discuss which treatments would be most suitable for you, before you are whisked off to the radiology department for chest and dental x-rays. If the purpose of your stay is simply to rejuvenate yourself, this may all seem a little extreme, but it is amazingly reassuring to return home knowing that your body is working as well as it can. And if it is not, at least you have found out what needs to be improved and how to do something about it.

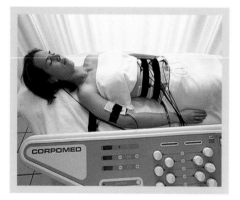

ABOVE: ELECTRONIC TONING PROVIDES AN ALTERNATIVE TO HOURS IN THE GYM

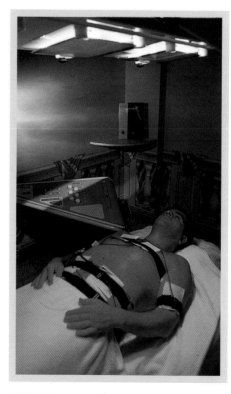

ABOVE: LIGHT THERAPY IS SAID TO ENHANCE HEALTH

ABOVE: PERSONAL TRAINERS ARE ON HAND TO PROVIDE ONE-TO-ONE PILATES TRAINING

The Beautymed treatments – which are carried out using futuristic-looking machines – are designed to tone up muscles while draining tissues of toxins and fluids. Corpomed helps fight flabbiness in the face and body by enhancing lymphatic drainage: a pulsator is attached to your ear and synchronizes the massage with your heartbeat. The Corpofit treatment sends electric impulses to acupuncture points on the face to prevent it from becoming droopy, while 17 minutes strapped to the Corpotrim belt (developed by NASA scientists for astronauts) is the equivalent of spending an hour doing aerobics. Once you have recovered from the culture shock, the gentle whirring of the instruments and the mild tingling of the electrodes is strangely soothing.

After this it is time for a body peel followed by a hydrotherapy massage with botanical oils. The therapists are all multilingual and excellent at explaining how and why each treatment works – which is essential, since it can all be somewhat bewildering at the start.

La Prairie skin products, which are used in all the facials and other beauty treatments at the Clinique, undergo rigorous scientific research and are among the best in the world. Along with the pampering, physical exercise is integral to the Rejuvenation and Beautymed programs. Aerobics and aquagym cater to all levels of fitness, while the gym instructors are specialists in devising custom schedules to promote rehabilitation after illness, accidents, operations or childbirth.

Although Clinique La Prairie is often booked up months in advance and almost always has a full quota of 40 guests, it sometimes feels as if you have the whole place to yourself. It is ethereally peaceful and appointments are scheduled so that guests rarely bump into one another in the corridors. When they do, they are often swathed in bandages from recent surgery. The Clinique is renowned for its discretion, but as everyone spends most of the day trailing around in fluffy white robes — which are great levelers — it is almost impossible to recognize anyone, famous or not. If people do meet in the communal areas, they are normally staying on their own and more often than not are part of the international jet-set.

Those bent on total anonymity can have all their meals in their room or suite. For the more gregarious, the dining room serves good and mildly exotic food — grilled chicken on a bed of rice and coconut milk, for example, or escalope of duck's liver fried with artichokes followed by ewe's yogurt and honey, accompanied by wine and coffee if desired. This is a prime place for people-watching, but if you are visiting the Clinique alone it is worth bringing a book, since sitting on your own can be lonely.

The Clinique is housed in two buildings; one is a large, old-fashioned chalet where the original rejuvenation treatments of the 1930s took place. The other is an ultra-modern reflective structure that houses most of the medical facilities. The bedrooms are large, if slightly impersonal, and many have balconies with spectacular views of the surrounding mountains and Lac Léman. There are mini-bars (without alcohol), fax machines and large Bang & Olufsen televisions equipped with cable channels and a VCR.

Clinique La Prairie is far too serious — and expensive — to be described as young and fun. However, for those in need of it the appliance of science works: after one week you are almost guaranteed to leave with glowing skin, a diminished waistline and improved energy levels.

CLINIQUE LA PRAIRIE
CH-1815 CLARENS-MONTREUX
SWITZERLAND
TEL: +41 21 989 33 11
FAX: +41 21 989 33 33
INFO@LAPRAIRIE.CH
WWW.LAPRAIRIE.CH

Daintree Eco Lodge & Spa, Queensland, Australia

Daintree
Eco Lodge & Spa,
Queensland, Australia

There are only a handful of resorts in the world where the spa experience starts well before you reach the treatment table. The Daintree Eco Lodge & Spa, hidden in 30 acres of the earth's oldest tropical rainforest in Queensland, is one such place. The sheer majesty and beauty of the surroundings combine to make you feel extraordinarily humble; the forest has existed for more than 110 million years and it is a true privilege to be able to visit such an unblemished environment.

This is a World Heritage National Park where there are more species of trees in five acres of forest than in all of North America or Europe. The site of the four-and-a-half-star Eco Lodge has been used as a resting place by the forefathers of the local Aboriginal tribe, the Ku Ku Yalanji, for many thousands of years because of its plentiful natural resources — fresh springwater, an abundance of edible and medicinal plants and wildlife. There are numerous bathing pools and the valley it lies in has its own micro-system, which means that the climate is comfortable.

The owners of the estate, the Mahoney family, all work on site and are highly conscious of their responsibility in maintaining the delicate eco-balance of the forest, the spa and the indigenous people. Plumbing and electrical cables are kept above ground, much of the power is solar generated and waste is recycled. The 15 stilted guest lodges are set back within the canopy of the trees like treehouses and blend in so well that it feels as though you are living right in the heart of the rainforest. There is no need for artificial sound effects or music here: the multitude of birds, frogs and insects create a symphony of their own that is far more lyrical and imaginative than anything recorded.

"When most of us look at the rainforest, we see a complex wall of green. But for traditional Aboriginals like our families, the rainforest is a kitchen, medicine chest, tool shed and a church."

KU KU YALANJI ABORIGINAL PEOPLE

The tranquil surroundings of the spa are seen very much as part of the restorative therapy to help guests who are feeling overstrained. The therapists work regularly on stress management and many of the treatments have been developed to help free the mind and soak away tension.

The spa successfully achieves this by integrating the wisdom and culture of the Ku Ku Yalanji into its ethos. It has developed a range of therapies that combine ancient indigenous medicines and massage techniques with aromatherapy, color therapy and herbalist principles. The treatments complement the numerous activities available while staying at the lodge — the Aboriginal Kodo body massage provides an ideal remedy for tired muscles after an extensive bush-trek, while 90 minutes of the Mala Mayi body treatment (including a local Mapi mud wrap and traditional Aboriginal scalp massage) after a long day on the reef will leave you feeling like a blissed-out zombie. Not that it matters, of course, because by that stage of the day you will be surrounded by a number of other equally blissed-out zombies.

RIGHT: COLLECTING MUD OCHRE

ABOVE: INITIATION INTO AN ANCIENT RITUAL

There are more than 20 therapies to choose from, most of which are carried out in one of the light and airy treatment rooms, where guests lie on a custom-made timber bed carved in the shape of an ylang-ylang leaf, with the music of the rainforest echoing around. Many of the ingredients in the preparations, such as wild ginger and rosella, have come straight from the forest and add an undeniable tingle-factor to the whole experience.

The Secret Sacred treatment is well worth traveling halfway round the world for. For women only, this once-in-a-lifetime experience is something never to be forgotten. After a short walk through the forest guests arrive at a sacred waterfall site where, for several millennia, Aboriginal women went to bathe and gather their medicinal plants. Guests are anointed with symbolic markings made from the mud ochers at their feet before being given a slow and meditative massage. This ritual to celebrate the female body, spirit and soul ends with a bathing ceremony in the cool waters of the pool beneath the waterfall.

DAINTREE ECO LODGE & SPA
20 DAINTREE ROAD
DAINTREE, QUEENSLAND 4873
AUSTRALIA
TEL: +61 7 4098 6100
FAX: +61 7 4098 6200
INFO@DAINTREE-ECOLODGE.COM.AU
WWW. DAINTREE-ECOLODGE.COM.AU

To avoid unnecessary damage to any of the rainforest, guests are always asked to keep to the strictly marked-out paths, and elevated wooden walkways connect the treehouses to the restaurant and the treatment areas. Each of the spacious air-conditioned treehouses has its own secluded view from a micro-screened balcony. Some even have an open-air spa jet-bath from which, covered in bubbles, you can watch the passing wildlife.

The wildlife is abundant. A birdwatcher's paradise, the Daintree Forest contains about 430 species of birds, many of which are regularly seen on the Eco Lodge property, including some rare varieties such as the Great Billed Heron, the Black Bittern, the Little Tern and the Beach Stone Curlew. The region has eight different wildlife habitats ranging from billabong and open grassland to mangrove swamps and riverbanks — all of which attract a staggering variety of creatures including metallic blue Ulysses butterflies, Hercules moths and flying foxes, to name but a few.

Some of the wildlife ends up on your plate. The Baaru House Restaurant perches above a freshwater lagoon, and guests can sit either indoors or outside on the balcony terrace illuminated by flaming torches. The food, which is splendid, mixes international cuisine with local organic produce. Breakfasts are a colorful mass of exotic fruits, yogurts and wattleseed muesli. Dinners can be as exotic as desired, with crocodile fillets in wonton sheets followed by kangaroo coated in wild thyme and then gumleaf bavarois with Kakadu plum jelly. The menus include an abundance of fresh seafood, while healthy low-fat options are always available. The chef is also happy to cater to special dietary needs such as diabetic and low sodium.

There is huge opportunity for adventure at the Eco Lodge, with scuba diving and snorkeling on the Great Barrier Reef, fishing on the Daintree River and day-long horseback-riding treks through the forest. Safaris to Cape Tribulation and Cooktown can be organized, as well as sunset river cruises. Most fascinating of all, though, are the guided Aboriginal Rainforest Culture Walks. This is the ideal way to peek into the past and see how the indigenous people learned to survive in the forest. You will learn which plants are medicinal, which insects are edible, and what vegetation was growing 600 million years ago and is still here today. Whatever reason brings you to the Eco Lodge, the experience puts things into perspective.

ABOVE: THE SPA IS DWARFED BY THE SURROUNDING MOUNTAINS

The West Coast of Ireland is so remote that even the Romans never managed to reach it. It remained stubbornly Celtic while the rest of Europe was colonized and, as a lasting reminder of this, Gaelic is still spoken in the area. The landscape is wild and desolate, with range upon range of barren hills, home to few but mountain hares and a handful of hardy, windblown sheep. It is a true wilderness.

Cradled below Mweelrea, the highest peak in the area, at the edge of an isolated lough, lies the Delphi Mountain Resort & Spa — a 500-acre forested estate that offers the overstressed a place to find some peace. It is so quiet that you can actually hear the silence — which can be an eerie sensation. Conditioned as we are to the ever-present background noise of cars, trucks, airplanes, cell phones and sirens that constantly assaults us in normal life, it takes a moment or two to adjust to the stillness of Delphi.

Delphi Mountain Resort & Spa
Leenane, Ireland

The isolation is all part of the cure. Frank Noone, one of the co-owners, describes why: "We figured that the long drive (it's four hours from Dublin or an hour and a half from Knock Airport) would be cathartic for guests. The further they had to come, the more stress they would be able to leave behind."

Rejuvenation comes in two forms. You can spend your days cocooned in the spa, being pampered from 10 A.M. to 6 P.M. Or, if you are feeling hyperactive, you can make the most of the activities offered at the adjoining adventure center and de-stress yourself by rappeling down vast climbing walls or kayaking through sea caves. Equally, you can have the best of both worlds and combine vigorous indulgence with vigorous exercise.

Delphi Mountain Resort & Spa, Leenane, Ireland

The atmosphere at Delphi is deliciously relaxed; you know you have arrived somewhere really special when a dram of Irish whiskey is recommended as a beneficial (but optional) part of the rejuvenation process.

There is, however, a wide range of more conventional treatments to choose from at the spa including nine different forms of massage and 14 beauty therapies. On the whole, guests usually ditch the decision-making process at reception and opt for one of the prearranged treatment bundles. For example, the popular 48-hour "Relax & De-stress" package incorporates aromatherapy and Indian head massages, reflexology, an enzymatic sea-mud wrap and relaxation classes such as yoga, t'ai chi, pranic breathing and qi gong.

Between treatments you can melt into one of the comfortable loungers in the circular relaxation area, sipping herbal tea or a glass of freshly squeezed fruit juice, while mulling over the panoramic mountain views outside the enormous windows.

Along with a Jacuzzi, sauna and steam room, the spa also has a hydrotherapy bath. This features high-pressure rotating underwater jets that briskly massage every inch of your body. Special seaweeds and lightly scented aromatic oils are added to the water to help you relax and detoxify, as well as to improve your circulation. The sessions normally last for about 15 minutes and, to help you unwind even more, multi-colored lights stream through the water, transforming it — and you — into vibrant shades of green, blue and pink.

Given Delphi's proximity to the sea, it is not surprising that marine-based products are used in many of the treatments. The algotherapy, during which you are enveloped in a mixture of micronized seaweed and warm seawater, smells mildly peculiar but is extremely good for detoxification. The Thalgo marine facial reoxygenates and brightens the skin, and is particularly recommended for smokers. The therapists at the spa are not only very friendly and approachable, they are also well informed and will give you useful tips on most subjects from wrinkle avoidance to coping with chronic back pain.

If you want to shape up as well as detox, you can train in the indoor sports hall. The one-on-one lifestyle assessment is a good springboard from which to launch a new fitness regime. It involves a thorough analysis of your eating habits, body composition (such as water content and fat percentage), strength, endurance and flexibility to give you a true measurement of your current fitness levels and also a realistic picture of what you should be aiming to achieve.

ABOVE: THE RIVER CORRIB RUNS THROUGH GALWAY CITY

ABOVE RIGHT: A TRADITIONAL CELTIC CROSS

You can view the landscape around Delphi Mountain Resort & Spa as either a bleak but beautiful wasteland or as a huge potential playground. The owners of the retreat regard it as the latter and started the "adventure" aspect of the business 16 years prior to opening the spa. Along with fairly standard activities such as mountain biking, tennis, circuit training, hiking and aerobics there is also rock climbing, sailing, surfing, kayaking and an aerial rope assault course that does wonders for your sense of balance. It looks indescribably scary from the ground but, once you are up there, it is enormous fun. Safety ropes connect you to overhead wires and, if you lose your footing, you fall all of two inches.

For those in search of more gentle pursuits there are stretching and meditation classes, as well as quiet walks around the lough and the forest. Dolphin-watching boat trips are regularly organized, providing you with a memorable opportunity to survey the scenery and spot wildlife.

The ultimate aim at Delphi is that you mix the spa treatments with physical exercise to help you tune out from the everyday worries of home. You are given as much time and space for personal reflection as you need and, as a result, the healing process kicks in very quickly.

It is also helped by the fact that you are staying in such comfortable surroundings, specifically designed to put you at your ease. The lodge is built of indigenous natural materials – rocks from the surrounding moors and timber from storm-felled trees. Taking inspiration from the mountains and the rivers, virtually every wall is curved, and walking down a corridor is like following a stream. An invitingly aromatic turf fire blazes in the reception area and its peaty aroma permeates the whole building.

DELPHI MOUNTAIN RESORT & SPA
LEENANE
CO. GALWAY
IRELAND
TEL: +353 95 42987
FAX: +353 95 42303
EMAIL: DELPHIGY@IOL.IE
WWW.DELPHIESCAPE.COM

Many of the 27 bedrooms are fashioned with just one type of wood such as beech, elm, oak or birch. The rooms are spacious and simple, with Shaker-style furniture and king-size beds. There are mini-bars (without alcohol) and televisions are available on request.

Losing weight is the only thing you will find difficult to do at Delphi. The food is healthy but opulent and it is hard to resist the temptations posed by soy-and-sesame-glazed quail with shiitake mushrooms, saffron-butter-poached monkfish with tomato and coriander tabbouleh, and roasted plum tart with thyme ice cream and hazelnut praline. The seafood is excellent and fabulously fresh, coming straight from Killary Harbour, where consignments of mussels and lobsters are flown daily to top Paris restaurants.

ABOVE: THE ENTRANCE TO THE LODGE AND SPA

The Hotel Gellért &
Gellért Spa Baths, Budapest, Hungary

Budapest oozes with history. One of the most beautiful cities of Eastern Europe, it also sits on a particularly porous part of the Earth's crust. Thermal springs bubble up throughout the metropolis (at the last count there were more than 118) and have played an important part in the country's cultural past. The Romans were the first to recognize the medicinal properties of the hot spas some 2,000 years ago and since then the Magyars, Turks, Germans and Russians have built bath houses in their vicinity.

RIGHT: THE HOTEL GELLÉRT WITH VIEWS OVER
THE RIVER DANUBE

Nowadays the spas still play an extremely important part in daily Hungarian life and are a focal point for socializing. Partly as a result of the ancient bathing traditions and partly as a consequence of the post-war communist government's policies the baths are egalitarian, open to everyone and remarkably inexpensive.

The largest and most famous of the spas is situated beneath a series of green copper cupolas adjoining the four-star Hotel Gellért. Built in 1918, this magnificent building stands on the banks of the Danube on the Buda side of the river (the capital was formed when two towns, Buda and Pest, were amalgamated in 1872). It houses three indoor thermal pools, as well as a large outdoor wave pool and a smaller thermal pool. The waters are reputed to be beneficial for sufferers of rheumatism and chronic degenerative joint and spine diseases as well as lumbago and neuralgia.

The thermal springs that supply the baths emanate from Gellért Hill, which stands behind the hotel. It was here that the Magyars murdered the martyr Saint Gellért by stuffing him in a barrel, ramming long nails into its sides and rolling it down the slope to the river below. Customer service has definitely improved in the intervening few hundred years, but it is still best described as unconventional.

ABOVE: THE INDOOR HEATED POOL

ABOVE: THE OUTDOOR POOL

While the Hungarians are very friendly to foreigners, their language is not. Related only to Estonian and Finnish, it seems utterly impenetrable. Mercifully, all the treatments at the Gellért Baths are explained in English, German and Russian, but apart from rudimentary pleasantries, the staff do not speak much English, although some are fluent in German.

In some ways, though, not knowing what to expect is all part of the fun. The therapy names alone (which include galvanization, carbon-acid tubs, medical gymnastics, mud treatments and underwater traction baths) are enough to send the imagination into overdrive. Unsurprisingly, all of these can be administered only with the approval of a doctor. However, the swimming pools, thermal pools, steam room and massages do not entail any such prerequisite and are a unique experience. The architecture and turn-of-the century interior design – a riot of vaulted ceilings, pillars, mosaics and Roman statues – emphasize the strong feeling of antiquity.

The first thing to remember is that it is essential to rent a bathrobe and a towel, otherwise you can end up trailing about in the cold wearing nothing but a wet swimsuit. The indoor swimming pool, with its high ceiling, green and blue tiles, Romanesque columns and lion's head fountains, is superb. The clientele, of all ages, swim in the same direction, in a rather stately aquatic procession that is strangely relaxing. The 30-meter (33-yard) outdoor pool, with its wave machine, is particularly popular with the young and has a much more boisterous atmosphere.

Before entering the thermal pools guests are issued a fairly unbecoming apron with which to cover themselves because, at this stage, it is time to drop the swimming costume. Having said that, the aprons are pretty useless and most people do not bother with them at all. If you feel awkward about wandering around nude, don't be. The area is filled with people of all shapes and sizes, and the whole spectacle is so mesmerizing that any initial embarrassment evaporates rapidly. The same is true of the massages (although nudity is not necessary here) which take place in a large room where up to 20 people can be tended to at the same time. There is a choice of four massages with typically blunt descriptions — hygienic, medical, talcum powder and foot. There is no soothing music, just the background chatter of the masseurs as they happily swap gossip.

The spa baths are run by the municipality, not by the Hotel Gellért, although entry is free for those staying at the hotel. They are open from 6 A.M. to 8 P.M., except for the weekend, when they close at 1 P.M.

The Hotel Gellért is renowned for its faded grandeur and is endearingly eccentric. Several years ago a writer staying there returned to her bedroom after a trip to the baths to find that the housemaid had enterprisingly oiled her electric typewriter with face cream. The concierge is equally helpful — the state-employed staff at the baths can sometimes be rather off-hand, so he will cheerfully advise on where else to visit for a massage that provides a little pampering.

The architecture at the Gellért is thoroughly eclectic — part Art Nouveau, part communist, and part baroque. The bedrooms range from utilitarian through faded splendor, with Art Deco marquetry and potted plants. The views from them are marvelous, although if you choose a room that overlooks the Danube it is worth bringing a pair of earplugs.

There are plenty of communal rooms including a brasserie, a crowded but jovial bar, a coffee saloon and a formal dining room where breakfast is served. This involves the usual assortment of cereals, breads and rolls, but with the added sparkle of an array of pickles and a model house made entirely of Trappist cheese.

LEFT: THE FAMOUS HOTEL GELLÉRT FAÇADE

ABOVE: THE ELEGANT ENTRANCE TO THE HOTEL GELLÉRT

ABOVE: THE HOTEL SERVES AN IMPRESSIVE SELECTION OF LOCAL WINES

The Hungarians have always enjoyed their food, but although it is good, it is anything but light. Menus at the Gellért include goulash soup with pearl barley and potatoes, followed by veal with cheese and béchamel sauce, potato croquettes, rice, carrots and cabbage strudel. Dauntingly, all this is served on one plate. The Gellért pancake is not for the faint-hearted either — filled with nuts and raisins, it is covered in a thick chocolate sauce. There are lighter versions, but if you venture out into one of the neighboring restaurants expect liberal doses of paprika, pork, goose-liver paté and cream.

While you are eating, particularly in the evenings, you will probably be serenaded by violin- and guitar-wielding gypsies. The locals generally tip them to make them go away.

Budapest is a city where poets are treated as national heroes and it has some of the best opera and music anywhere in Europe. It is also a sightseer's mecca; you will want to make time to see the parliament buildings, the Citadella fortress, the Matthias Church and Saint Stephen's statue. Heroes' Square, the Old Post Office Savings Bank, the Gresham Palace and the Franz Liszt Music Academy are equally memorable.

The Hotel Gellért and Spa Baths may not have the slick service and customer care of other top-end luxury resorts, but it has charm and unapologetic originality, and these are more than enough to make it worth visiting.

HOTEL GELLÉRT
1111 BUDAPEST, SZENT GELLÉRT TÉR 1
HUNGARY
TEL: +36 1 385 2200
FAX: +36 1 466 6631
RESOFF@GELLERT.HU
WWW.DANUBIUSGROUP.COM/GELLERT

The Alpine slopes below the towering peak of Mont Blanc harbor one of France's better-kept secrets: Megève, an unspoiled hamlet seemingly untouched by the passage of time. In the winter dark wooden chalets with low-slung roofs huddle under a blanket of pristine snow, lacy ribbons of smoke drifting from their chimneys, while sleigh-pulling horses stand patiently in the village square, munching in their feedbags. In the summer the place is awash with color; wildflowers adorn the mountainsides and hollyhocks, daisies and peonies sprout riotously from innumerable gardens and window boxes.

Les Fermes de Marie, Megève, France

ABOVE: IN WINTER MEGÈVE IS A POPULAR SKI RESORT

Of course, time has not really bypassed Megève — it has just been well managed. Property developers have not been allowed to go berserk with concrete and, as a result, the area retains the charm it has had since the 1920s. What is truly remarkable is that much of the village has been created only within the past 20 years. At the heart of this lies Les Fermes de Marie, one of the best spas in the Alps.

A hamlet within a hamlet consisting of nine cabins straight from Hansel and Gretel connected by a series of underground corridors, Les Fermes de Marie was built by Jean-Louis and Jocelyne Sibuet. Jean-Louis spent five years scouring the Savoy countryside for dilapidated old farmhouses and then transported them back to Megève, where they were painstakingly reconstructed piece by piece and turned into a 69-bedroom four-star hotel with an adjoining spa known as the Beauty Farm.

A relaxed, friendly and low-key atmosphere pervades Les Fermes de Marie (named after the Sibuets' daughter) and the spa is a favorite of many French families — with children of all ages — who come back to stay year after year. It is also one of the few places where dogs are welcomed with open arms.

ABOVE: BOULDERS TAKEN FROM THE SURROUNDING
MOUNTAINS FRAME THE INDOOR/OUTDOOR POOL

"While husbands play golf, go rafting or ski – depending on the season, of course – wives can catch up on their sleep, spend a day at our spa, play a game of tennis or go shopping."

JOCELYNE SIBUET

The natural elements of earth, wind, fire, water and stone have provided Jocelyne with the inspiration for the interior design of the Beauty Farm. Hundreds of smooth, round, glaciated granite boulders, which are said to radiate healing energy, are incorporated into its walls. They complement the bare-timber open rafters and paneling that make up the rest of the spa. This establishes a relaxing, rustic ambience, ideal for unwinding.

This is a place to come and be spoiled. The spa specializes in beauty treatments and Jocelyne has spent the past 15 years developing and perfecting a range of herbal skincare products based around the plants growing in the adjacent meadows and mountains. "I am passionate about herbal treatments," she says. "When you live in the mountains, surrounded by wildflowers, you can't help it." The resulting concoctions are delightfully aromatic, and positively melt into the skin.

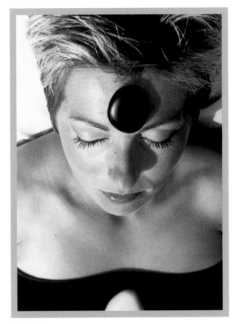

ABOVE: NATURE PROVIDES THE INSPIRATION FOR
THE SPA'S PRODUCTS

ABOVE: LOCAL EDELWEISS IS USED IN
THE BEAUTY PRODUCTS

ABOVE: STONE THERAPY – A TREATMENT IN WHICH
THE SPA SPECIALIZES

Horsetail, gentian, oat milk, arnica, edelweiss and hazelseed oil are all variously included
in the treatments, and the spa specializes in body wraps. The oatbran-and-clay wrap, in
particular, improves the circulation and helps detoxification. It is a surreal experience:
you are left to doze gently in what appear to be soft packs for 20 minutes as the gloopy
mixture gently cooks away any poisons.

The Beauty Farm also specializes in stone therapy. As you lie on a bed of warm rounded
stones in one of the 20 treatment cabins, a therapist uses hot basalt pebbles to massage
tense muscles. These are alternated with cold marble pebbles to relieve tense nerves.
It is blissfully relaxing, leaving you feeling at peace with yourself and with life.

Guests at the spa are offered a number of different packages ranging from 90 minutes to
six days. Other therapies include lymphatic drainage, Thai massage, auto-heating mud
packs, reflexology and aromatherapy. In the unlikely event that guests can drag themselves
away from the treatment table, there is a fully equipped gym as well as an indoor pool,
hydro-massage bath, sauna and Jacuzzi.

Walking into Les Fermes de Marie is like stepping into a Walt Disney fairytale set where almost everything is made of warm, glowing wood and looks as if it has come straight from a gingerbread house. There are low ceilings, open log fires, comfortable sofas bulging with cushions and reassuringly eccentric pieces of furniture originally salvaged from local farms and now lovingly restored by Jean-Louis. Throughout there is a simple country-style theme — in the library, the paneling over the chimneypiece comes from an old pair of doors and in the main dining room a hayrack is now used to display antique cheese-making equipment. This is not to say that Les Fermes lacks sophistication — far from it.

The attention to detail is more than impressive. Each bedroom is completely distinct from the others — different fabrics are used, some beds have canopies while others have no adornments but a traditionally carved pine headboard — but every one is unfailingly cozy and welcoming. The rustic touch does not mean a loss of technological comforts such as refrigerators, televisions and climate control — simply that everything is discreetly and decoratively hidden.

LES FERMES DE MARIE
CHEMIN DE RIANTE COLLINE
74120 MEGÈVE
FRANCE
TEL: 00 33 450 930 310
FAX: 00 33 450 930 984
CONTACT@C-H-M.COM
WWW.C-H-M.COM

In the same way that natural ingredients from the surrounding countryside are incorporated in the beauty products, if something grows locally and is edible it will probably appear on a menu in one of the three restaurants at Les Fermes — Le Restaurant Gastronomique, La Rôtisserie and Le Restaurant des Spécialités Fromagères. The food is good, although the menus veer towards the heavy side with such delicacies as duck foie gras roasted in buckwheat, crayfish from Lac Léman with black truffles followed by Savoy cake *cuit au moment* with dairy-farm ice cream and fruit marmalade. Children are in their element as they can have their supper separate from the adults, secreted away in a den hidden under the eaves.

Megève is a popular destination for families not simply because of its untarnished setting, but also because there are so many things to do. In the winter there is good but relatively uncomplicated skiing. For those who need more of a challenge, Chamonix beckons a little further up the valley. In the summer there is hiking, horseback riding, fishing and even the chance of a private airplane flight over the crystalline glaciers of Mont Blanc.

The Sibuets were determined that guests should feel completely at home, and they have succeeded. After a long day at the slopes followed by a massage, you think nothing of collapsing in front of the fire with a mug of hot chocolate in one hand and a piece of cake in the other.

ABOVE: MOUNT BATUR IN THE CENTER OF BALI

The Legian
Hotel & Spa, Bali, Indonesia

Despite itself, Bali has become the honeymoon capital of the world. It is not surprising really — this small Hindu island in the middle of the Indian Ocean is blessed with a tropical climate, scenery of unparalleled beauty, including a range of volcanoes, and a native population whose charm and friendliness is legendary.

ABOVE: A VIEW FROM ONE OF THE BEDROOMS

Part of the Indonesian archipelago, Bali in the 1930s was considered the hippest hangout in Asia for hedonists and artists. Ornate and colorful temples stand on every corner, highlighting the fact that the Balinese are very focused on their religion.

Bali may have evolved over the years, but there are still many wonderful places to stay on the island. For sheer sensuous luxury the Legian Hotel at Seminyak is hard to beat. Standing right on the edge of the ocean, it provides a world of peaceful indulgence, where everything — from the architecture and the food through the spa and the setting — has been chosen to give pleasure. As you meander along its paved walkways you cannot help but lose yourself in the sound of the sea, the rich smell of the frangipani trees and the soothing coolness of the breeze. Your senses become heightened and your appreciation of your surroundings increases day by day.

The new spa pavilion, with its thatched roof and floor-to-ceiling windows, is set in the hotel's beautiful South Gardens. Looking straight on to the sea and surrounded by lotus ponds and palm trees, it is the essence of tranquility. And, attuned to the romantic disposition of many of its guests, more than half of the treatment rooms are designed to cater specifically for couples.

ABOVE: A TREATMENT ROOM

The spa at the Legian focuses on one thing: restoration of body and soul through sensuous pampering. Massage has played a part in Balinese culture for centuries and no visitor should leave without experiencing the unique national version, which combines muscle stretches, long stroking movements, skin rolling and pressure-point manipulation. It can be very gentle or quite vigorous but, unlike other therapies such as shiatsu, it is very relaxing and does not leave you feeling stiff or bruised the next day.

In contrast, a traditional Thai massage can leave some feeling very stiff. The spa is one of the few places in Bali that specializes in this treatment, which, like the Balinese variety of massage, is based on a blend of pressure-point stimulation and stretching. The difference with a Thai massage is that the therapist really gets to work on deep tissues and the result is the equivalent of a head-to-toe workout. It is not in the least relaxing, but is tremendously invigorating. Wearing comfortable cotton pyjamas, you lie on thick floor mats while a fragile-looking therapist defies all probability by kneading and stretching you with a strength and intensity that ought to be impossible for someone so slight.

The spa has two other signature treatments. One is the warm stone massage in which smooth rocks are placed on the body's energy points to relax the muscles and create a feeling of well-being. Equally soothing is the Ayurveda shirodhara therapy, which starts with some gentle Ayurvedic stretching before a soft stream of oil is poured onto the "third eye" area of the forehead. Although predictably messy (mercifully each of the five treatment rooms has its own private shower attached), this ancient ritual is both calming and rejuvenating.

Many spas all around the world offer treatments similar to those at the Legian, but the little thoughtful touches are what sets the Legian apart from the rest. There are exotic scented flowers in all the treatment areas and bathrooms; a pedicure or manicure includes a whole arm or lower leg massage as opposed to the standard foot or hand rub; the products used in the facial treatments are all handmade using fresh, natural ingredients. Even the gym is special: as you pound away on one of the high-tech machines you look out through a window as big as a wall onto a beautiful manicured garden.

RIGHT: A BALINESE MASSAGE IS A SENSUOUS EXPERIENCE

Everything about the Legian is aesthetically stimulating. The architecture has a carefully thought-out symmetry, emphasized at night by sophisticated lighting systems that transform the place into a magical 1920s film set. The two-tier pool, which is cobalt blue by day, miraculously turns emerald green once the sun has set and every room is designed so well that it looks as if it has come straight from the pages of an interior design magazine.

Those staying at the hotel are given not just a bedroom but an entire suite. There are 70 of them and they abound with little luxuries. Each has a small but fully equipped kitchen with a microwave and a refrigerator full of tempting goodies. The marble-clad bathrooms have more fluffy towels than could ever be used in a day, as well as an endless supply of fragrant bath treats. The floors are all parquet and the beds all queen-size four-posters. On the balconies there are sumptuous daybeds to lounge in, and at night, if you are staying in one of the elevated suites, it is tempting to ignore the humidity and throw open the sliding doors to let the light sea wind swirl around you.

The Legian has employed one of Germany's top chefs, Dorin Schuster, to take charge of its kitchens. Having been head chef in several Michelin-starred restaurants before moving to Bali, Schuster's cuisine can only be described as excellent. The menus, which are a fusion of Eastern and Western styles, change regularly and feature a combination of fresh seafood and locally grown produce. The hotel has a lavish and tempting list of imported fine wines.

If you venture out of the peaceful confines of the Legian, you will not be short of things to do. The island is a favored destination for enthusiastic surfers, but for underpopulated beaches go to Lovina on the northern coast where the volcanic sand is black. Ubud, in the fertile heartland of the island, is the best place to explore Balinese culture. The shops here sell authentic carvings and art instead of the mass-produced factory objects found in Kuta.

Kuta is a seething town close to the Legian, and is worth visiting just to experience its sheer vibrancy. But beware: if you buy goods in the market and they are placed in a red bag, it is a sign to other shopkeepers that you are a soft touch. Bargain for everything, and if your purchases end up in a black bag you will know you have earned the traders' respect for being a tough customer.

ABOVE TOP: SEATING AREAS ALLOW GUESTS TO SOCIALIZE

ABOVE: ONE OF THE TRADITIONALLY DESIGNED BATHROOMS

THE LEGIAN HOTEL AND SPA
JALAN LAKSMANA
SEMINYAK BEACH
KUTA, BALI 80361
INDONESIA
TEL: +62 361 730 622
FAX: +62 361 730 623
EMAIL: LEGIAN@GHMHOTELS.COM
WWW.GHMHOTELS.COM

There is something marvelously decadent about sitting on a Caribbean beach and sticking a flag in the sand beside you to signal to the waiters that you would like another drink.

ABOVE: THE LESPORT COMPLEX

LeSport, St. Lucia West Indies

LeSport sounds as if it would be terrifying to anyone who is not a dedicated athlete — a list the length of your arm is put up on a noticeboard each morning giving details of the day's activities. These can include volleyball, cycling, tennis, aerobics, water skiing, windsurfing, golf and archery. If you have the energy, you can be on the move constantly from 7 A.M. to 7 P.M. Supplementing all the jumping about and running around, there is also LeSport's spa, the Oasis, which perches above the rest of the resort on the top of an emerald-green forest-covered hill.

LeSport, on the northwest tip of St. Lucia, offers the ultimate "body holiday" with exercise, pampering and luxurious comfort set against a lush tropical backdrop. Nevertheless, how you interpret "body holiday" is up to you and if you do not feel like moving an inch, you do not have to do anything other than lounge in the sun, have a treatment or two at the Oasis and then spend the evenings sipping cocktails at the Piano Bar. Equally, if you would prefer to shift weights in the gym all day or learn how to do t'ai chi, the facilities are there for you to do so.

There are two things that make LeSport different from nearly every other spa. First, it is almost a money-free zone. You choose a package that suits you and virtually everything — two sessions a day at the Oasis, food, drink, accommodation and sports tuition — is included in the price. This leads to the second point: the unlimited alcohol results in what can only be described as a very jolly atmosphere.

ABOVE: THE OASIS

Many of the stress-management classes take place on the beach, where the waves and wind enhance the general calming effect. LeSport has expert instructors in t'ai chi, qi gong, yoga and meditation. Again, all levels are catered to, although the teachers are particularly good with beginners. There are regular talks and lectures on stress reduction, as well as the opportunity for individual consultations. However, one of the simplest ways to unwind is just to set the alarm clock for 6:45 A.M. and join the early morning power walk, illuminated by the first rays of the sun rising on the horizon, along the beach and in the hills.

There is one thing about the Oasis that cannot be avoided – the flight of 79 steps that lead up to it. However, once at the top you are rewarded by the sight of a Moorish palace (based on the design of the Alhambra Palace in Spain) with verdant gardens, terraced gazebos and landscaped ponds. This elegant setting houses 25 treatment rooms including six for massage, two for aromatherapy and four for Chandra head, neck and shoulder rubs. There is also a gym, a sauna and hot and cold plunge pools, as well as the relaxation temple, which looks out on to a tranquil lily pond.

Unless a special program has been arranged, the day will not be filled with spa treatments; depending on the package you have chosen, there will be just two or three. At the start of each stay a nurse will check weight and blood pressure and then work out a suitable regime. The Oasis is good on details and if you are traveling with someone then the other person's treatments are organized to coincide with yours. On this note, newlyweds should sample the Honeymoon Massage, when you not only receive a full-body massage but are also taught how to give one to your partner.

Broadly speaking, the Oasis offers two program types from which to choose classes – exercise and stress management. These sessions can be mixed and matched, depending on your physical and mental state. In the exercise bracket there are classes for all levels (and versions) of step, aerobics and aqua aerobics, along with circuit training and weights in the gym. Personal trainers are on hand to give one-on-one sessions should the need arise.

Give us your body
for a week and
we'll give you
back your mind."
LESPORT MANTRA

One of the reasons why LeSport is so successful in helping guests to rejuvenate is that you cannot help but rise to the challenge. Perfect your stroke during a tennis lesson, work on your drive at the nearby St. Lucia golf club, or even learn something completely new like fencing or sailing. There are so many opportunities to do new things that it becomes difficult to say no to anything — and the more you do, the more your mind relaxes.

Scuba diving is one such activity that is a shame to miss. A variety of Professional Association of Diving Instructors (PADI) qualifications are taught, ranging from the most basic through Assistant Instructor level. Those who have achieved the first stage can go out on one of the many dives around the island to see firsthand the diverse marine life, the vibrant coral reef and the remains of several shipwrecked vessels.

LeSport caters to a wide spectrum of guests, from honeymooning couples to mothers and daughters enjoying a bonding week (children usually have to be over 16, although from the end of June to the end of September the age limit is 12). With the multitude of group activities and various in-house entertainment options in the evenings, the resort is commendably welcoming for those who are traveling alone. In fact, LeSport is one of the few places that offers a range of bedrooms at special lower rates for the single traveler.

The 154 bedrooms, including a number of
suites, all have air conditioning and private
terraces, but no televisions. The designs are
based on the interiors of West Indian
plantation houses, with four-poster beds
and rattan furniture. You can have breakfast
in bed but all other meals are served either
in the Clubhouse (justifiably proud of its
full-blown afternoon teas); in the open-air
dining room, Cariblue, for "cuisine légère";
or in TAO, the feng shui-ed East-West
fusion restaurant. There are always
low-calorie options available, and the
Deli serves up a good range of healthy
sandwiches. If your weight is not a
consideration there is plenty of chocolate
cake, and the Piano Bar stays open —
literally — until the last person goes to bed.

LESPORT
CARIBLUE BEACH
PO BOX 437
CASTRIES, ST. LUCIA
WEST INDIES
TEL: +758 450 8551
FAX: +758 450 0368
TROPICHOL@AOL.COM
WWW.LESPORT.COM.LC

The Mansion Hotel Spa, Werribee, Australia

The demands of international business mean that many people regularly fly around the world and end up staying in bland, characterless and, quite frankly, unmemorable hotels. As increasing numbers of stressed businessmen and women have found, performing at your best after a long flight and a night in an uncomfortable, strange bed is almost impossible. This has fueled the rise of designer retreats, personalized boutique-hotels with all the pampering of a first-class spa in a luxurious place, but equipped with advanced communications facilities to meet every executive need.

The five-star Mansion Hotel, just a 30-minute drive from the heart of Melbourne's main business area, is one such place. Opened in 2000, the 92-room retreat occupies a wing of the historic Werribee Park Mansion. There is a marvelous feeling of release as you leave the built-up areas of Melbourne and turn into the long gravel drive of Werribee Park. Suddenly it seems as though you have entered an English country estate with its rolling parkland dotted with landscaped trees and bushes. The giraffes, rhinos, antelopes and zebras wandering freely through the grounds in the distance are something of a surprise (the State of Victoria's Open-range Zoo takes up much of the parkland near the hotel), but they only add to the sense of escape.

The surprises continue once you arrive at the Mansion itself. Built by a pair of Scottish immigrants in the 1870s, it is a huge monument to Victoriana. The wing that is now the Mansion Hotel was added in the 1920s and was once a seminary. From the outside it is traditional in design. On the inside it is an interior designer's heaven — a sea of chrome, glass, light, stone and space. This is cutting-edge aesthetic chic.

Diving into the swimming pool at the spa feels almost sinful. The surrounding architecture is so geometrically perfect that anything as wobbly as the human body seems somewhat out of place. However, the clean lines and cool slate are remarkably conducive to clear thinking and peace of mind. The rest of the spa is designed in a similar style, with the advanced cardiovascular equipment in the gym ideal for working off any rage caused by a difficult business meeting.

For more gentle ways to de-stress you can select a 90-minute aromatherapy or deep-tissue full-body massage, although the latter treatment is almost as vigorous as going to the gym. There are a series of beauty therapies to choose from that all use the chemical-free Jurlique product range. But, for sheer indulgence, an hour-long hand massage and manicure with essential oils is hard to beat. You come out of it feeling ridiculously pampered.

However, those who want serious spoiling should devote their stay to the Tranquility Package. This is sensuous extravagance in the extreme: seven hours of pampering that starts with a soothing yoga session focusing on breathing and gentle stretches, followed by a Vichy shower exfoliation and a firming body wrap. This is followed by reflexology and a scalp massage and is finally topped off with an aromatherapy facial and a hand treatment. To keep the wolf from the door, a series of freshly squeezed fruit juices and tantalizingly healthy snacks such as seasonal fruit muffins and fresh salads are supplied throughout the day.

There are various exercise classes including aerobics, stretch, yoga and mini-circuits. The Mansion Hotel also has six floodlit tennis courts where you can play after the working hours have ended. Professional tennis coaches are available for up to a whole day's instruction. Equally, a personal trainer who is on hand in the gym will happily take you for a run, up to 8 kilometers (5 miles) long, on one of the jogging tracks around the park.

The building that houses the Mansion Hotel may once have been a seminary, but former ordinands would have difficulty recognizing their past home. "We wanted to create a feeling of country, but with a contemporary, slick edge," says architect Roger Wood. The interior is now blisteringly sophisticated — celadon-colored glass walls separate bedrooms from their en-suite bathrooms, fitted out with stainless steel benches and chrome taps. Needless to say, amenities such as in-house movies, mini-bar, safe, modem and fax access are standard. The rooms are simple, Zen-like and uncluttered; neither romantic nor cozy but eminently comfortable.

Throughout the hotel the design concentrates on reflective lighting and imaginative use of texture and color, set off by elegant contemporary furniture. It is peaceful to spend an hour or two playing chess in the library, or frame of snooker in the large billiards room. Joseph's Bar and Joseph's Restaurant, both named after the seminary wing, are hip and inviting. The cuisine is inspired by rustic Italian cooking, with specialities including Parmesan Reggiano with pickled vine tomatoes, grilled garfish with tomato, and espresso, walnut and vanilla affogato. The attention to detail — in service, quality and presentation — is exemplary but, since the chef, Barry Vera, has worked extensively with top restaurateurs such as Marco Pierre White and Terence Conran, you expect nothing less.

What you do not expect is an on-site vineyard. A short stroll around the corner from the hotel is the Shadowfax winery and vineyard. This is worth visiting even if only to admire the innovative design of the building, which, despite having a rusted sheet-metal exterior, blends in remarkably well with the surrounding area. You can eat here and buy wines straight from the cellar.

The park around the hotel presents a strange dichotomy. In parts it is an exotic Never Never Land with its vines and unusual wildlife; elsewhere it is rural England with its ornamental lake, croquet lawn, archery and cricket on the Great Lawn. Within the same environs is the Victoria State Rose Garden, which boasts more than 4,500 bushes arranged in the shape of a giant Tudor rose. In sum, the place is extraordinary, and consequently provides the perfect antidote to the rigors and stresses of business life.

THE MANSION HOTEL AT WERRIBEE PARK
K ROAD
WERRIBEE, VICTORIA 3030
AUSTRALIA
TEL: +61 3 9731 4140
FAX: +61 3 9731 4001
SPA@MANSIONGROUP.COM.AU
WWW.MANSIONHOTEL.COM.AU

The Mayr Health Spa,
Lake Wörth, Austria

Not all spas involve indulgence and pampering. Some of them don't even make you feel well. In fact, if you're not feeling considerably below par by your third day at the Mayr Health Spa, then something is going wrong. But, bearing in mind the mantra "no pain, no gain," you can rest assured that by the time you leave its serene environment you will be feeling — in both body and spirit — light-years better than when you arrived.

With the Carinthian Mountains providing an impressive backdrop, the Mayr Spa stands in a golden valley on the shores of Lake Wörth in southern Austria. Founded in 1976, it promotes the theory that the key to good physical and mental health lies in maintaining a healthy digestive system — years of eating the wrong food does untold damage to the whole body. The result is a medically supervised detoxification system based on the teachings of Dr. Franz Mayr (1875-1965). He believed that a well-functioning digestive tract is created by three factors: fasting to regenerate the system; cleansing by taking base salts, drinking lots of water and having abdominal massages to restore the body's correct pH balance; and education to improve eating habits, including how to chew food properly.

This spa is run along traditional lines, with guests coming from all over the world for a cure and not for luxury. Not that the Tyrolean-style Mayr is uncomfortable — far from it. But it does have a slightly schoollike feel to it. Each day is governed by strict routine, guests don't have a choice about what to eat and there is a fairly fearsome "Health Program" rule book that includes the instruction to drink the morning dose of bitter-tasting Epsom salts "cheerfully."

"Death lurks in the intestine" is quite a scary thought and creates enough of an impetus to make you pay close attention to the initial examination given by the house medical director, Dr. Harald Stossier. After checking your posture, blood pressure, eyes, tongue, teeth and gums, he then palpates your abdomen. With his fingers alone he can tell immediately if your liver is enlarged (due to overwork), if your diaphragm is out of place or if your intestines are inflamed. Most of us suffer from one or all of these conditions. He then prescribes a treatment regime based around your detoxification requirements.

The programs last between one and four weeks, and in some cases guests end up eating nothing but special bread rolls, milk and yogurt. Generally, those staying for a short period are put on what is termed the Mild Purification and Drainage Diet. This basically involves existing on a challenging diet of stale spelt-flour rolls, sour milk, plain vegetable broth, steamed vegetables, herbal teas and boiled potatoes.

The bread rolls are stale on purpose — to make you chew properly. By the time you leave the clinic, you will have perfected the art of chewing a single roll for 30 minutes. The spa's logic is that badly chewed food is hard to digest and, in order to give the digestive tract a chance to relax, everything swallowed has to be completely liquefied. The spa mantra runs something along the lines of "drink what you chew, and chew what you drink."

Regular doses of Epsom salts and bicarbonate of soda mean that trips to the bathroom are frequent, so don't be surprised if you have to leave one of the exercise classes in a hurry. You are also encouraged to drink huge amounts of water and by the end of each day you may well have consumed up to seven liters.

One of the common results of the detoxification process is what the spa refers to as a "crisis." In other words, you react against the toxins being expelled from your body and start to feel headachy, tired, bad-tempered, depressed and sometimes nauseous. It usually passes within two or three days, but if you are having problems dealing with your crisis the doctor may issue you with a do-it-yourself enema kit — which is enough of a challenge to take your mind off any other issues.

At the Mayr, it's not just a case of what and how you eat, but when you eat. The days start and end early — guests are encouraged not to watch television and to put lights out by 9 P.M. so that the body can relax completely and have the best opportunity to regenerate itself. The evening meal, which is frugal by any standards (sometimes just herbal tea and honey), is eaten at 6 P.M. As the days go by, it can be difficult to predict if you will feel hungry or not — some people are absolutely ravenous, others seem to be able to exist on the meager diet with few problems.

The daily ritual includes as much exercise as you can face, from gentle stretching and yoga to jogging round Lake Wörth or cycling. The spa has a small gym, three saunas and an indoor swimming pool, but summer guests often find it more invigorating to take a plunge into the lake. Austria's second oldest golf course, the 18-hole Dellach, adjoins the spa.

After breakfast guests undergo a Kneipp bath to improve circulation. This involves plunging various bits of your body first into hot water for 5 minutes and then immediately into cold for 30 seconds; each day focuses on a different part of your anatomy, from feet through to hips. A massage follows, which is more therapeutic than pampering. You are packed off before lunch to lie in your room with a warm liver-compress — actually just a hot-water bottle wrapped in a towel, but very soothing nonetheless.

THE MAYR HEALTH SPA,
GOLFHOTEL AM WÖRTHERSEE, GOLFSTRAßE 2,
A-9082 MARIA WÖRTH-DELLACH
KÄRNTEN, AUSTRIA
TEL: +43 42 73 25 110
FAX: +43 42 73 25 11 51
FLIGHTS: AUSTRIAN AIRLINES

Since education is an important part of the Mayr program, there is a question and answer session with Dr. Stossier in which he explains the digestive cycle and the roles that various organs and different foods play in it. Guests are also encouraged to attend the cooking demonstrations led by head chef Peter Mayr. His recipes, involving no white flour or sugar and minimum fat, are inspirational. The intention is to provide you with the information you need to keep your body on an even keel once you have returned home. It is extremely inspiring, although maintaining the spa's strict dietary regime can be difficult in normal life — many people are still at work at 6 P.M., when according to the Mayr schedule it is time to sit down to dinner.

Palazzo Arzaga, Brescia, Italy

History, culture, indulgence and an 18-hole championship golf course: the Palazzo Arzaga has all the right ingredients to make it the perfect place for a romantic getaway. The fifteenth-century monastery has been converted into a luxurious hotel with a sumptuous spa attached. So while the girls are being pampered, the boys can disappear onto the fairway for an hour or two — or vice versa, of course.

ABOVE: ANTIQUE FRESCOES ADORN THE MAIN STAIRCASE

At the end of a long avenue of trees, the Palazzo is just 10 minutes from Lake Garda and 30 minutes from Verona. Surrounded by a beautifully landscaped estate, which includes two golf courses, a twelfth-century chapel and a series of pine-scented walks in the woods, it has been restored to the highest standards and offers a secluded haven of peace from the frantic tourist areas around Lake Garda. Original frescoes from the fifteenth century (which had been covered with plaster for hundreds of years and were only rediscovered during the renovations) adorn the walls in some of the bedrooms and communal areas, adding to the feeling of otherworldliness that hits you as soon as you arrive.

It would be very easy not to leave the environs of the Palazzo at all: apart from the spa, it has a shop, three restaurants and a series of ground-floor interconnecting salons that include a library, music room, drawing room and bar. But staying put would mean missing out on a host of other entertainments such as the world-famous opera in Verona and the fabulous shopping in Mantua and Milan, not to mention the sightseeing in Venice, only an hour away.

ABOVE: SHIATSU MASSAGE

ABOVE: THE SLIM AND TONIC POOL

ABOVE: A "BIG DRIVE" MASSAGE

The Saturnia Spa, which is run by the same organization that owns the renowned Terme di Saturnia in Tuscany, is located on the ground floor and basement of the Palazzo Arzaga. Many guests visit the spa in order to lose weight, and the programs skillfully mix pampering with medical supervision to ensure that you make the most of your stay.

Treatment packages range from two days to six days, and at the start of any regime there is a consultation with the in-house physician, Dr. Marco Merlin. His approach concentrates on scientifically proven methods combined with a realistic assessment of human nature — basically, he is not going to starve you! The kitchens, while serving a wealth of delicious but nonslimming fare, also provide a parallel menu of light meals. Dr. Merlin consults directly with the chefs to make certain that the food you are served is consistent with your program.

Many spas ask you to wear paper underwear during your treatments, but this is Italy and at the Palazzo you are issued with a paper thong instead. Once the shock of this has faded, you are whisked off for a session in the thermalion machine, an enclosed, bathlike capsule from the top of which your head pokes out. You are heated up and then squirted with jets of hot and cold water. It is the most bizarre sensation, but is said to help the circulation. After that comes a trip to the indoor "slim and tonic pool," where the water is packed with a cocktail of magnesium, potassium, sodium and iodine — all of which are said to stimulate the metabolism and lymphatic system and help diminish cellulite.

Massage plays an important part in the programs and there are more than ten treatments to choose from, among them Ayurveda, reiki, lympho-drainage and the four-handed "Big Drive," which consists of two therapists massaging in complete synchronization. However, if the opportunity arises of a shiatsu massage with Florian Lene, seize it with both hands. He once worked as a trainer with the Romanian national athletics team and he can bend your body into shapes that you would never have dreamed possible and dissolve knots in your muscles that you did not even know existed.

Not all the treatments are focused on slimming; there is a good selection of beauty therapies including mud wraps, facials, skin peeling and anti-wrinkle remedies, including Botox injections.

PALAZZO ARZAGA
25080 – CARZAGO DI CALVAGESE DELLA RIVIERA
BRESCIA, ITALY
TEL: +39 030 680 600
FAX: +39 030 680 6270
INFO@PALAZZOARZAGA.IT
WWW.PALAZZOARZAGA.COM

The Palazzo Arzaga has all the comforts you would expect in a five-star hotel. The design throughout is sophisticated and elegant, with antique mahogany furniture and classical paintings. There are 84 bedrooms, ranging from elaborate suites through more modest rooms in the Golf House. The latter have much less character than those within the Palazzo — although that's not surprising, since it is hard to beat the experience of sleeping in a room where the fresco-covered walls are works of art in themselves.

From the architecture to the food, the ingrained culture and history of Italy pervades every minute of your stay at the Palazzo. The menus are based on traditional recipes — pea and squid risotto, pasta with porcini and truffles, steak au poivre and local cheeses from Brescia and Bergamo. The light menu involves whole-grain bread rolls with fresh salads or soup followed by steamed sea bass or grilled lamb and then perhaps ricotta cheesecake with raspberry coulis. In the surrounding area there are good restaurants in Desenzano, a small port on the edge of Lake Garda.

A trip to Verona is essential. The setting for Shakespeare's *Romeo and Juliet,* it has a wonderful open-air Roman amphitheater where operas are performed in the summer. It is also a shopaholic's dream boasting, among many others, Prada, Gucci and Fendi for clothes and accessories, and Domotex for homeware. A 20-minute sail from Desenzano will take you to the medieval town of Sirmione with its twelfth-century fortress — one of the finest examples left in Europe. Also worth exploring is the nearby wine-growing area of Franciacorta with its caves and numerous vineyards.

If you are only staying at the Palazzo for a weekend, you will find it almost impossible to fit everything in. Apart from the golf, the spa and the sightseeing, there are also morning ecological walks and t'ai chi and yoga sessions, along with aerobics, stretching and water gymnastic classes. You can play tennis or go horseback riding in the surrounding woods and hills, or just visit the small but well-equipped gym. There is almost too much to do here and so, to make the most of your trip, the answer is just to try a little bit of everything.

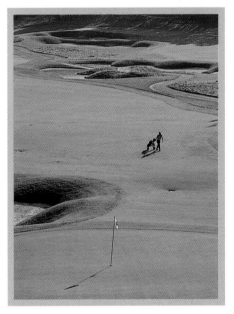

TOP: SAN VIGLIO ON LAKE GARDA

ABOVE: THE 18-HOLE GOLF COURSE IS ONE OF THE BEST IN ITALY

ABOVE: THE HYDRO POOL WITH ITS ASSORTED JETS, SHOWERS AND BUBBLE SEATS

Traveling is normally exhausting, but there are few things more uplifting than arriving at your hotel in time to watch the sun setting over the Dead Sea. On the banks of this natural wonder is the Mövenpick Resort and Sanctuary Zara Spa, so close to the shore that, as the lights of Jerusalem begin to twinkle across the glittering water, you can wander down to the sea and wallow in the warm mud, or simply lie back and float in water that supports you like an armchair. Weariness dissolves immediately.

Sanctuary Zara Spa, The Dead Sea, Jordan

This is the Valley of Salt, the lowest place on earth at 400 meters (1,300 feet) below sea level, where the Dead Sea separates Israel from Jordan. It is also the home of the Sanctuary Zara Spa, a mosaic-tiled haven that is cradled in the middle of a traditional Arab village resort. It is the perfect place for a health and beauty retreat where access to unpolluted water and mud is limitless. It is so hot in the summer months that the thermal springs running into the sea evaporate as quickly as they arrive, leaving a rich residue of minerals.

These minerals — including magnesium, potassium and calcium chloride — are believed to be advantageous to health, benefiting in particular the immune system, circulation, detoxification and skin disorders such as eczema. Even the air is different — ozone rich and high in oxygen content due to the lack of altitude, it is said to contain extra UVA and UVB filters that allow a greater exposure to the sun with a reduced risk of sunburn. That said, you have to be really dedicated to sunbathe in a climate where, at certain times of the day, the heat from a flagstone is enough to burn naked skin.

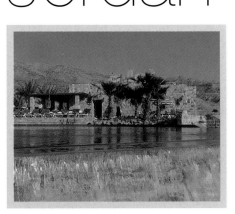

ABOVE: THE MÖVENPICK RESORT

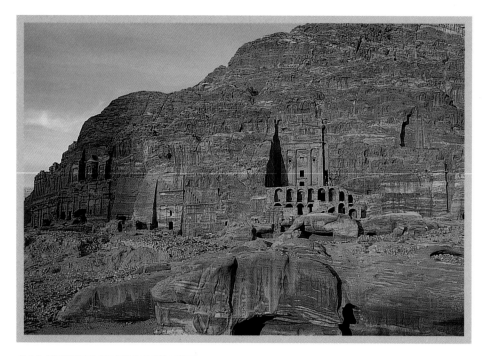

ABOVE: THE HISTORIC NABATAEAN CAVES AT PETRA

The Sanctuary Zara Spa is exactly what it says it is — a sanctuary from the heat and the stress of everyday life, where worn-out guests can rejuvenate themselves in the most luxurious of surroundings. A wellness clinic rather than a pure health spa, it is run by the same team that owns the Sanctuary in London's Covent Garden.

The reception area, with its gently bubbling fountain, emanates an atmosphere of cool tranquility. There are pools everywhere, enclosed by canopied terraces, each one offering a different form of hydrotherapy. The hydropool, with its pummeling jets of water and rimless edge overlapping the sea behind, makes you feel as if you could swim gently to Jerusalem. Alternatively, you can relax under a tropical rain shower scented with mint or enjoy the de-stressing effects of the indoor Dead Sea pool with its 23 percent concentration of salt water.

To gain the maximum benefit from the surroundings the therapists recommend that you spend ten minutes in Dead Sea water

ABOVE: STONE THERAPY

about five times a day – this helps your body to fully absorb the minerals that it needs. Equally, it is essential to drink plenty of water in order to help the detoxifying process.

There are more than 70 therapies to choose from, but the spa's signature treatment – the Dead Sea Salt Scrub– is definitely worth trying. Lying in one of the diamond-shaped treatment rooms you are rubbed with giant granules of salt mixed with essential oils to slough off dead cells. It is

scary how much comes off, but it leaves your skin, elbows and knees included, feeling unbelievably smooth. Equally impressive are the Dead Sea mud wraps. Coated from head to foot in purified green or black mud mixed with various oils and herbal extracts, you gently bake away the toxins. The most sublime experience, however, is the dry flotation and aromatherapy massage. Bizarre as it sounds, you are wrapped up in plastic and warm towels, then the table below you suddenly melts away, leaving you

floating in balmy water as one of the therapists gently massages your face.

A few words of warning: the salt concentration in the Dead Sea is far stronger than anything you are likely to have experienced before. Any cuts or rashes will sting horribly on contact with it, although mitigating this, they do heal up remarkably quickly afterwards. Above all, avoid getting water in your eyes because the pain can be excruciating, particularly if you are wearing contact lenses.

Despite the fact that the Mövenpick Resort opened only in 1999, it feels much, much older. The inspiration for its design came from ancient Jordanian desert villages, and as you wander along its courtyards and alleys, lined by two-story sandstone and mud houses, it feels as if you have stepped back in time. The simple facade, however, hides a sophisticated interior, which befits the resort's five-star status. Each of its 230 bedrooms has air conditioning, satellite television and a marble-encased bathroom, plus a balcony overlooking the sea or a garden. The lavish use of rich textiles, traditionally designed furniture and haunting Islamic art adds to the exotic *Arabian Nights* ambience that permeates your stay.

The man-made stream that flows from a fountain inside the hotel's main lobby winds down to the heart of the village, where most of the entertainment takes place. There are nine restaurants and bars, including Luigi's and Chopsticks, which serve Italian and Asian food respectively. Themed evenings happen at the buffet restaurant, Al Saraya, while the Grill serves traditional Middle Eastern cuisine, such as platters of mezze with hummus and tabbouleh, followed by red snapper and herbs. You can happily undo all the good work at the Spa by visiting the Valley Café and Bar for generous helpings of ice cream. After dinner you can make your way to the Romanesque amphitheater where nightly entertainment is laid on, including belly dancing and singing. You even have the option of smoking apple- or strawberry-scented tobacco through elaborate water pipes.

Whether you are staying at the resort for two days or two weeks, you will want to make time to visit the surrounding area. Jordan is one of the most historically significant places on earth. Mount Nebo, visited by Moses shortly before his death and possibly his burial site, is about 40 minutes away, as is the country's capital, Amman. The ancient city of Petra, carved from rock 2,000 years ago by Nabataean traders, is a three-hour drive away; its most famous building, the Treasury, was immortalized in the Hollywood film *Indiana Jones and the Last Crusade*. Recently opened to the public is the settlement of Bethany (20 minutes away from the Dead Sea), where archeological digs have uncovered fourth- and fifth-century writings confirming that this is where Christ was baptized.

MÖVENPICK RESORT AND SANCTUARY ZARA SPA
SWEIMEH
DEAD SEA ROAD
PO BOX 815538
11180 AMMAN
JORDAN
TEL: +962 5 356 1111
FAX: +962 5 356 1122
E-MAIL: RESORT.DEADSEA@MOEVENPICK.COM
WWW.MOVENPICK-DEADSEA.COM

Les Sources de Caudalie
Bordeaux, France

Only in a fantasy world would you ever dream of having a bath in wine or of being slathered from head to toe in a Merlot wrap. Only in France would this fantasy become a reality.

Buried in the heart of the Bordeaux wine-growing region, Les Sources de Caudalie is the world's only vinotherapy spa, where the healing properties of the grape are extolled and not only can you drink the Chardonnay, but also immerse yourself in it. This spa is truly a family affair — it is situated on part of Smith Haut Lafitte vineyard owned by Daniel and Florence Cathiard, and it is their daughter Mathilde who has been the driving force behind its creation.

ABOVE: ROLLING VINES SURROUND THE SPA

Each year Mathilde helped her parents during the wine harvest when they would gaily throw away tons and tons of discarded grapeseeds and pulp. A chance meeting with Professor Vercauteran of Bordeaux University stopped Mathilde in her tracks. "Do you know that you are throwing away the best part of the grape?" he asked, before going on to explain that grapeseeds contain polyphenols. His research had shown that polyphenols are extremely effective antioxidants, ten times stronger than vitamin E in fighting one of the body's greatest natural adversaries — free radicals.

Found in cigarette smoke, sunlight and pollution, free radicals are believed to play a contributory part in the onset of cancer and are certainly responsible for much skin damage associated with aging. Working with Professor Vercauteran, Mathilde and her husband, Bertrand, developed an extremely successful line of grape-based skincare products. A few years later, when the family discovered a 500-meter-deep hot spring on an undeveloped part of the estate, Mathilde knew that this would be the ideal spot for a spa.

The "French Paradox" has baffled doctors for years — how could the nation eat a diet high in cholesterol and yet, as a populace, suffer from a relatively low incidence of heart disease? The answer, it appears, lies in the antioxidant properties of red wine. Whether this is true or not, Les Sources de Caudalie claims that its vinotherapy regime (which includes imbibing a glass or two of the red nectar) will leave you feeling better and looking younger. It will certainly leave you feeling fabulously relaxed.

RIGHT: THE WINE-INFUSED BARREL BATH

The spa, housed in a rustic building made from pale wood and terracotta tiles, exudes an air of tranquility – instead of piped music your treatments are accompanied by the sound of birdsong outside. The design inside is light, stylish and unfussy, with panoramic views of the undulating vines, the turrets of the eighteenth-century château and the small ornamental lake.

You may be reclining in a purple-hued whirlpool bath, catching glimpses of young men working on the vines but, thanks to the clever design of the slatted windows, while you can see out, no one can see in.

This is not, however, a place to come and get fit, although there is a body-temperature pool and a tennis court enchantingly set amongst the vines. Instead, the spa offers three different types of treatment: anti-aging, which includes vino-lifts; slimming, which targets cellulite and restricts you to just 500 calories per meal; and relaxing, in which guests simply enjoy the massages and the French scenery, while eating and drinking like royalty.

A typical day will start with a Barrel Bath – a relaxing soak in a mixture of heated water from the spring, grape extract and essential oils, at the end of which you feel as if you have been gently marinated. After this you are led to the tisanerie (the herbal tea room) for one of the calming red wine infusions. By the time you reach the wrap stage, when you slow-cook for 20 minutes in a warm paste of wine yeast extract, Bordeaux honey and organic essential oils, you are positively floating. As if this were not enough, a facial follows, using a crushed-grapeseed scrub and mask. This is then topped-off with a grapeseed oil full-body massage. By this point you feel so relaxed that it is a miracle if you can remember how to walk.

In reassuringly Gallic fashion, food at Les Sources de Caudalie is taken very seriously and if you abstain from dessert and wine during your meals the waitresses are apt to look heartbroken. However, everything is so delicious that it is nearly impossible to refuse either. The four-star hotel next to the spa includes two restaurants — the brasserie-style Table du Lavoir and the gourmet version, La Grande Vigne. Both are overseen by chef Didier Banyuls — recipient of two Michelin stars. Many of his recipes, with their delicate use of garlic, olive oil and tomatoes, betray a strong Catalan influence. There is very little use of cream or butter and, despite being slightly more spartan than the gourmet versions, the low-calorie options are mouth-watering. Amazingly, a three-course meal of duck carpaccio, veal with spring vegetables and melon sorbet still amounts to only 500 calories.

Didier's wife, Maire-Louise, is an acclaimed sommelier and oversees a 10,000-bottle wine cellar that boasts some of the best vintages in France, along with a selection of tantalizingly rare cognacs. Guests are encouraged to take part in regular wine-tasting sessions at the nearby chateau. However, if you are absolutely determined to resist the food and drink and are instead bent on detoxifying yourself, you can embark on a one- to seven-day grape-fast during the harvest, which runs from September to November.

LES SOURCES DE CAUDALIE
CHEMIN DE SMITH HAUT LAFITTE
33650 MARTILLAC
FRANCE
TEL: +33 557 838 282
FAX: +33 0557 838 281
VINO@CAUDALIE.COM
WWW.CAUDALIE.COM

The pale cream hotel, although finished only in 1998, gives the impression of being much older and blends in well with the surrounding countryside. The interior is a model of bohemian chic. Every one of the 23 bedrooms and six suites is decorated differently, but each is gloriously romantic with a liberal scattering of antiques and chintz bed linen. The honeymoon suite, a stilted cabin overlooking the lake and its resident swans, is addictively comfortable.

Les Sources de Caudalie is a favorite with chic French couples who arrive en masse on the weekends, confirming that this is definitely a place to savor *à deux*.

Malaysia is a country rich in diversity and ancient healing rituals. Nowhere is this more apparent than on the tranquil island of Pangkor Laut, where a unique Spa Village nestles on the shoreline, surrounded by 300 acres of untouched rainforest.

ABOVE: THE PRIVATE ISLAND OF PANGKOR LAUT

Spa Village, Pangkor Laut, Malaysia

This is healing at its most exotic and luxurious. The influences of Japanese, Chinese, Malaysian, Indian and Thai cultures are evident throughout the resort in the astonishing attention to detail, the continual sensuous pampering and the timeless elegance of the architecture.

Situated in the Malacca Straits off the west coast of Malaysia, this is a tiny, privately owned paradise that is so perfect it ought to exist only in the imagination. The beaches are pearl white, the sea blood warm and the sunsets almost mystical. On arrival at the jetty, you are welcomed with garlands of flowers and brightly garnished coconuts brimming with chilled milk. An orchid is placed on your pillow each night and hibiscus flowers sprinkled over your bathwater — this is a place for indulgence where guests come to give themselves up to pure sensuality.

Nature is never far away. Traditional Thai massages are given in huts overlooking the sea, where the ritualistic art of relaxing in herbal steam — "prakop" — combines with the music of the ocean and the breeze to uplift the psyche. The island resounds with the calls of macaws, hornbills, frogs and monkeys, and the resident botanist enthusiastically leads regular trips deep into the forest. The Spa Village garden produces many of the ingredients used in the myriad different herbal treatments that combine to make this a resort dedicated to nurturing body and soul.

There are so many different treatments available at Pangkor Laut that guests are often at a loss as to which to choose. To simplify things, three umbrella programs have been developed: rejuvenation and longevity; beauty and slimming; or relaxation and stress reduction.

For example, the Spa Village's enlivening signature Traditional Treatment starts with a flowered foot wash and a Chinese foot pounding. After this you are escorted to the Bath House for a Malay herbal steam treatment followed by a Shanghai scrub that leaves every nerve-end tingling. Next, there is a Malay massage that consists of long kneading strokes and acupressure. The essential oils used have invigorating qualities to aid circulation. Massages can be taken in a conventional treatment room or under an open-air canopy, accompanied by the gentle tunes of wind chimes.

There are eight treatment rooms with private outdoor decks that are perfect for couples wanting to experience their programs together. There are also three herbal healing huts – Chinese, Malay and Ayurvedic – where you can watch the preparation of herbs, as well as receive consultations and treatments from the respective healers. In addition, the Wrap House has space for five people to luxuriate in restorative seaweed and Malaysian Kao Ling body wraps.

The rolling waves of the sea provide the perfect backdrop to the yoga pavilion, where group classes are taught t'ai chi, qi gong, meditation and gentle stretching. For those feeling more energetic there is a well-equipped gym in Royal Bay (about 400 meters/yards along the coast from the Spa Village), along with three all-weather tennis courts and two squash courts. One of the most memorable experiences is swimming in the "edgeless" pool as the sun sets. As you gaze at the horizon, the waters of the pool and the sea appear to merge seamlessly, creating the impression that you are immersed in an infinite lake of liquid gold.

Between treatments sustenance can be found at the Spa Restaurant. This is open for breakfast, lunch and dinner and serves a combination of European and Eastern foods. The choice is spectacular and the presentation is so artistic that it almost seems a sin to delve into the mounds of fresh fruit, breads and seafood on offer. If you are feeling too relaxed even to reach the restaurant, fresh juices, power drinks, herbal elixirs and light snacks can be served direct to your daybed down on the private beach.

SPA VILLAGE
PANGKOR LAUT RESORT
32200 LUMUT
PERAK, MALAYSIA
TEL: +605 699 1100
FAX: +605 699 1200
WWW.PANGKORLAUTRESORT.COM

Refreshingly, the beauty of the island has not been compromised by any of the building developments, primarily because the design of each building has been thought out carefully to ensure that everything blends in sensitively with the surrounding environment.

There are three different areas to stay in. The Spa Village has 22 guest villas, including the perennially popular sea villas, which stretch out from the shore on stilts. Each has been built to provide maximum privacy, but the walls of the bathrooms slide back so that you can experience the slightly surreal effect of relaxing in a scented bath while watching the fishing boats bobbing past in the distance. Around the corner, in Royal Bay, villas perch on the hillside surrounded by jungle, while others are scattered below among the colorful plants of the tropical garden. On the other side of the island there are private retreats known as the Estates. These exclusive hideaways have personal chefs, butlers and even personal trainers so that you can create your own unique idyll.

"This place is enchanting – it is paradise. This morning, when I woke up, I went out and I was moved, almost crying, to see what beautiful things God had done!"

PAVAROTTI

TOP AND BOTTOM: STILT HOUSE INTERIORS

MIDDLE: THE POOLSIDE BAR AND RESTAURANT

The Malaysian-style rooms are all blissfully comfortable with king-size beds and panoramic views. Each has air conditioning, a refrigerator and a CD player. Wherever you choose to stay, however, it is worth remembering that guests are firmly recommended to keep their villa doors shut. Not for security reasons – purely because the monkeys have a penchant for the complimentary banana shampoo supplied by the resort and are happy to steal it, and anything else they can get their hands on, to play squirting games with.

There is plenty to do on Pangkor Laut – the Water Sports Center provides snorkeling, scuba diving, water skiing, sailing, fishing and sunset cruises. There are seven bars and restaurants dotted about the island, but any indulgence can be walked off during a jungle trek, taking in the picturesque Emerald Bay, one of the most memorable beaches in the world.

This is, without doubt, a honeymooner's dream universe where luxury, privacy and tranquility are the watchwords.

Have you ever wondered what it is like at the edge of the world? An hour's drive from Manzanillo airport lies El Tamarindo, one of the most remote and exclusive spa resorts in the world. Utterly secluded, completely private and staggeringly beautiful, it is one of Mexico's best-kept secrets.

El Tamarindo,
Manzanillo, Mexico

At the end of a 7-kilometer (4-mile) private drive that winds its way through coconut and banana plantations, mountains and forest, El Tamarindo looks out over the Pacific, surrounded by 2,000 acres of tropical jungle with 15 kilometers (9 miles) of unspoiled coastline. This is the Costalegre, where, 500 years ago, the Spanish Conquistadors first landed. With its secret beaches and hidden coves, this stretch of coast has changed hardly at all during the intervening centuries.

Overlooking a white crescent-shaped beach, and set among palm groves, stand 29 thatched bungalows – known as palapas – that provide guests with luxurious accommodation and total isolation. Staying here is akin to living on the ideal castaway island – a teeming host of wildlife, including racoons, hummingbirds and huge-eyed lemurs, darts from bush to bush in the lush vegetation, while the sea is welcoming and the beaches ideal for sunbathing.

Nothing is too much trouble for the staff. Whatever you want, they will do their utmost to make it happen – whether you wish to have dinner à deux on the beach or at the end of the private pier, or have a massage in the jungle, it will not be a problem. Physically and mentally you have no choice but to switch off – cell phones do not work here and there are no televisions. Instead, guests make do with an 18-hole championship golf course carved from the jungle or spend time in sybaritic bliss at the spa hut.

ABOVE: A TRADITIONAL PALAPA

El Tamarindo, Manzanillo, Mexico

In the late afternoon on Tuesdays and Saturdays, a Temascal ritual is held at El Tamarindo in a specially constructed igloo-style sauna made with bricks of clay, piloncillo sugar and medicinal herbs. The Temascal is a pre-Hispanic tradition that invokes the healing powers of water, plants, air, earth and fire. Lasting for two and a half hours, it starts outside with the haunting sound of a seashell being blown. Next, guests anoint themselves with a scented mud containing coconut, cucumber and papaya, before taking a dip in the sea and afterward drinking fragrant herbal tea. Guests then enter the Temascal hut for the first of three 20-minute steam sessions to sweat out tension and stress. As the heat builds up, the sweet aroma of the herb-infused bricks pervades the atmosphere — peculiar, but uplifting.

The more conventional spa hut is set back in the forest, out of sight, but within earshot of the Pacific. It is blissfully tranquil with no noise but the continual birdsong, the occasional animal grunt and the regular lapping of the waves on the beach. There are no set appointment times for treatments — guests just select the one they want and choose a time that suits them. There are a number of healing massages including reiki, shiatsu, mahakari and chakra balancing, which all last between 60 and 90 minutes. A shorter relaxational massage for the back, head, neck and shoulders is ideal for relieving stiffness after a couple of rounds of golf.

The spa has a unique range of beauty products made with fresh, natural ingredients from the surrounding area, incorporating cucumber, aloe vera, lime and coconut. The beauty treatments include exfoliating mineral-mud wraps, papaya and sea-salt scrubs and aromatherapy facials. The spa staff are very laid back and massages are available in your villa, by the pool or even on the beach.

There are daily qi gong classes in the mornings followed by mediation sessions that combine various different philosophies ranging from Vipashana and Zen through to Shambhala and Judaism. The late afternoons are taken up with a medicinal form of yoga designed to restore vitality and engender a feeling of well-being.

TOP: THE RUGGED COSTALEGRE

MIDDLE: A TREATMENT ROOM IN THE SPA HUT

BOTTOM: THE RESORT'S INFINITY POOL

El Tamarindo, Manzanillo, Mexico   121

ABOVE: THE BAR ON THE FAIRWAY

The rustic palapa dwellings are the epitome of stylish comfort. There are four different settings to choose from — in the garden, in the forest, surrounded by palm trees or ocean facing — and each has the luxury of its own pool, Jacuzzi, air conditioning and private terrace equipped with large, comfortable loungers. In the evenings it is deeply relaxing to laze on one of these, with a margarita in one hand, listening to the sounds of the jungle. If you are lucky you may see an armadillo or a wild boar, or even catch sight of an elusive jaguar. At night the beach suddenly bursts into life as hundreds of small orange crabs rush from the sea to their holes and back again.

In keeping with the easy-going atmosphere at El Tamarindo, guests can choose to eat almost wherever they desire. There is a terraced, candle-lit restaurant, which serves an aromatic combination of Mexican, Italian and Asian cuisines; but for something more intimate the private dining terrace outside your palapa is perfect. Trays of avocados, chilies, sun-dried tomatoes, garlic and various other fresh vegetables are brought to each table so that guests can choose the ingredients for salsa or guacamole, which is then mixed on the spot. Freshly caught tuna or king prawns are grilled on a coconut-husk barbecue in front of you before being whisked straight on to your plate.

The layout of the resort is cleverly designed and there is so much space that you need never see any of the other guests if you do not want to – it is a honeymoon heaven. Equally, for those who want to socialize there is always a friendly atmosphere down by the main pool or in the bar.

The golf course is renowned as one of the best in Mexico, with breathtaking scenery and an imaginative layout. But because the resort is so isolated, very few people know about it and, consequently, you can play an entire round without seeing another soul. The thirteenth hole is so secluded that you might consider a quick dip in the sea below it. Between the ninth hole and the tenth there is a small thatched café that serves cold drinks and fortifying snacks and even provides cold towels.

If you are not fanatical about golf, there are memorable walks to take through the forest, as well as kayaking, diving, snorkeling and mountain biking. It is also well worth visiting Playa Teopa to watch scores of hatched turtles returning to the sea.

EL TAMARINDO
KM 7.5 CARRETERA MELAQUE Y PUERTO VALLARTA
CIHUATLÁN
MEXICO
48970
TEL: +52 315 351 5032
FAX: +52 315 351 5070
WWW.LUXURYCOLLECTION.COM

Family holidays can end in tears. No one ever wants to do the same thing: toddlers are apt to have embarrassing tantrums in public while teenagers either disappear completely or descend into boredom-induced sulks; parents, meanwhile, are usually simply exhausted and in need of a rest.

BELOW: GUEST VILLAS SET AMONG THE TREES

Thermae del Parco, Santa Margherita Di Pula, Sardinia

One place that manages to cater to everyone's whims is the Forte Village Resort in Sardinia. This 55-acre resort, situated on the southeast corner of the island, is a cross between the Garden of Eden and the Land of Oz. Protected from harsh north winds by a range of mountains, it has its own subtropical microclimate, and its lush gardens and pine woods are tended by an army of cheerful gardeners. Nothing, including the pristine beaches and azure Mediterranean, is more than a ten-minute walk away.

Designed more or less to mimic an Italian village, it has eight dazzlingly luxurious hotels, the grandest — the Cala del Forte — consisting of six suites with a private butler. There is a series of spacious bungalows set among the pines, where guests can have breakfast served on their private terraces.

Surrounded by a serene Japanese garden is the Thermae del Parco. This is one of the few areas in the village that is a child-free zone and so is the perfect place for parents to retreat to while their offspring are being entertained elsewhere. One of Europe's top spas, it specializes in thalassotherapy.

Thalassotherapy is the combination of two Greek words meaning "sea" and "medical treatment." It involves the medicinal use of heated seawater to restore health and vitality, and is particularly beneficial to those suffering from circulatory problems, water retention, arthritis, stress or fatigue. The theory is that when fresh seawater is heated to a certain temperature it opens the pores, allowing the body to absorb minerals from the water.

The five thalassotherapy pools at the Thermae del Parco should be visited in strict rotation. The water in the first pool, which is heated to 38°C (100°F) has a density higher than that of the Dead Sea. It is also chocolate brown and somewhat oily, owing to its extraordinarily high magnesium content. Although a surreal experience, bathing in it is not entirely relaxing – you cannot submerge yourself unless you are really determined, and the salt content makes even the smallest abrasions sting intensely.

The remaining pools have diminishing salt and temperature levels, but contain an increasing number of jets and waterfalls that are delightfully invigorating and particularly effective at massaging away strained muscles. The final pool is similar in salinity and temperature (20°C/68°F) to the sea and brings the 90-minute session to a close. Along the way you will probably spot one or two international soccer players receiving treatment for sports injuries – the waters are said to benefit joints and bones so much that even Russian astronauts come here to recover from voyages into space. For those who are not quite such high achievers, it is still deeply relaxing and therapeutic.

In the second pool guests can have an underwater shiatsu massage, which is sublime. Lying on your back, your body supported by the mineralized water, you gaze up at a cloudless blue sky and listen to the tinkling of a waterfall. A therapist gently manipulates your limbs, allowing the water to massage you while focusing on your shiatsu pressure points. Once loosened up in the pools, you can unwind even further in the Romanesque sauna and mosaic-rich Turkish bath.

The wealth of more than 50 health and beauty treatments includes massages, salt peels, wraps and facials. Treatments take place in rooms dotted about the gardens, with walls of one-way glass though which you can see but no one can look in. For an even more sybaritic experience, you can have a four-handed massage lying on the grass outside, protected by walls of thick vegetation.

The spa has a team of specialists including doctors, dieticians, personal fitness trainers and physiotherapists who will formulate personalized programs depending on the length of your stay. There is a high-tech gym, as well as daily aerobics and aqua aerobics classes. To visit the spa you have to be a guest in the Forte Village Resort.

Forte Village Resort teems with things to do and positively welcomes children of every age. There is a Mini Club for children age 2–11. A supervised play area, it is full of climbing frames, toys and even a little train that collects children in the morning and brings them back in the evening. The Junior Club caters specifically to 12–17 year olds and provides a daily menu of fun activities including canoeing, Ping-Pong and soccer. There is also an electronic games room and a restaurant dedicated entirely to kids – which is noisy, messy and extremely popular.

The village contains nine swimming pools, 12 tennis courts, a soccer field, a mini-zoo, a shopping arcade and even a church. The multitude of watersports offered includes sailing, diving, water skiing, windsurfing and snorkeling. Retail-therapy junkies are not deprived of their fix – the shops are filled with designer labels, such as Versace, Ralph Lauren, Zegnia and Mont Blanc, to name but a few. The guests are generally very well heeled – they need to be because, while Forte Village Resort is bliss, it is expensive bliss.

However, it does offer safety, space and entertainment. As one guest succinctly put it: "There is a perfect mixture of seclusion and independence when wanted, but activities and organization when desired. It is costly but it is worth it."

LEFT: THE BEAUTIFUL SARDINIAN COASTLINE

ABOVE: THE SAUNA

Meal times are especially indulgent affairs. There are 18 restaurants (although some are only open at certain times of the year). The range of cuisine covers all tastes. At the Belvedere you can expect to sample good Italian food with a twist, such as spaghetti with sea urchins and dried mullet roe. You will find spit-turned roasts at the Brazilian eatery, pan-fried red mullet in black olive sauce at Mediterraneo, pizza and hot dogs at Planet USA and roasted suckling pig at Sardo. There is a plethora of rich ice creams and sticky treats on offer to keep anyone with a sweet tooth more than happy. Do not go to the resort expecting to lose weight — there are far too many temptations.

As soon as you pass through the front gates of the Forte Village Resort, you enter a parallel universe and the chances are that you will not want to leave it. Most families, if they can afford it, come back year after year.

LE MERIDIEN FORTE VILLAGE
SANTA MARGHERITA DI PULA
09010 - CAGLIARI - SARDINIA
ITALY
TEL: +39 070 921 71
FAX: +39 070 921 246
FORTE.VILLAGE@FORTE-HOTELS.COM
WWW.LEMERIDIEN-FORTEVILLAGE.COM

There are many spas in the Alps, but none is quite like the remote Therme Vals in Switzerland. At the end of a deep valley in the Swiss canton of Graubunden, 1,200 meters (4,000 feet) above sea level, it stands half-buried in the mountainside. At moments it is difficult to work out where the building ends and the mountain starts.

The Therme Vals has a strange history. Its therapeutic hot spring has been a magnet for tourists since the 1800s. However, more recently the spa facilities and the adjoining hotel became so dilapidated that only the most hardened enthusiasts came to visit, and bankruptcy loomed. The village community took matters into its own hands in 1983 and united to buy the Therme and the hotel outright. It then took a gamble and employed the architect Peter Zumthor to redesign the spa completely.

His ideas were revolutionary and there were a few hiccups along the way. Well into the construction of the new quartz stone and concrete facility, someone in the local pub suggested that the powerful thermal water would "dissolve the stone like Alka-Seltzer." No one had thought to test it.

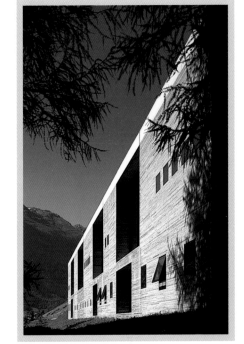

Luckily all was well and the result is a veritable work of art — a concept-based spa, with flowering meadows growing on its flat-topped roofs. Zumthor took his inspiration from quarries and water flowing spontaneously from the ground, and his building bears absolutely no resemblance to any traditional Alpine chalet. However, such is its impact that within two years of completion it had been classified as a historic landmark. It is now a place in which to luxuriate and rediscover the primal experience of bathing.

Therme Vals,
Vals, Switzerland

"A fascination with the mystical properties of the stone world inside mountains, with darkness and light, with light reflected on water or radiating in steam-filled air, a delight in the singular acoustics of bubbling water in a world of stone, a feeling for warm stones and naked skin, for the ritual of bathing — these are the ideas that inspired us."
Peter Zumthor

The Therme has a certain primordial feeling to it and yet everything — from the baths and the corridors to the unadorned windows and doorways — has a precise geometry that is almost bunkerlike in its simplicity. The walls consist of layer upon layer of locally quarried Valser quartzite blocks — 60,000 of them in all, each laid by hand. Many of the ceilings are made from cantilevered concrete slabs with small fissures between them that let the light in and yet, paradoxically, make you feel as if you are bathing in a cave deep in the heart of the mountain. These combinations of light and shade, open and enclosed spaces and linear elements make for a highly sensuous experience.

The complex is entered by means of an underground tunnel where the rich iron content of the Valser water first becomes apparent as it pours from wall-mounted copper pipes and stains the stone beneath. There are seven pools to choose from, both indoors and out. They range in temperature from a steamy 42°C (107°F) "fire pool" to a cold-plunge pool at 14°C (57°F). The scented flower pool is deeply sensuous, while the harmony pool brings a whole new meaning to the concept of rock music – igneous "music" is filtered through the walls and if you submerse yourself in the warm water you can still hear it reverberating gently around you.

Below the pool deck is a wellness center where guests can have treatments focusing on relaxation and pampering. The spa's signature treatment is the Chi Yang therapy, which is a combination of acupressure, relaxation and beauty massage using essential oils mixed with particles of 22-carat gold. This is said to harmonize cell function and leave the skin looking radiant. There is also a caviar power facial – DNA gel is extracted from fish roe and used in moisturisers as an anti-aging weapon. For the less adventurous, there is a raft of more conventional treatments including aromatherapy, kelp wraps, facials, manicures and pedicures.

Therme Vals, Vals, Switzerland

The Hotel Therme Vals adjoins the baths. Made up of several different buildings, it is a triumph of 1960s tourist architecture — towering, flat-roofed apartment houses with repetitive facades and not a single piece of wood. It is endearingly awful. Its directors refer to it as their "zero-to-five-star hotel."

Over the years the complex has undergone several piecemeal renovations — all in different styles. The result is that parts of the hotel are worn out and others are so outdated that they have come back into fashion again. It is hilarious. As Peter Zumthor puts it: "The brown panels on the roof and balconies, originally painted navy blue, are vaguely reminiscent of wood. In the main building a few pieces of antique-style furniture look utterly lost on the imitation-stone tiles of the hallways and corridors. The bedrooms, most of them furnished in the styles of the '80s and '90s, illustrate various responses to what guests supposedly or actually find pleasing."

Even so, its eccentric charm more than makes up for what it lacks in conventional style. Surprisingly, the food is rather good. There are two restaurants. Lucullus specializes in fresh international cuisine and also provides a 1,000-calorie-a-day diet for those who have chosen to do a week-long weight-loss and detox program. The other restaurant, Chessi, focuses on regional foods such as local smoked meats accompanied by sweet and sour pickled vegetables, followed by cream polenta with Valser lamb ragout, with bread-and-butter pudding or iced nut gateau for dessert. There is just one caveat — do not try swimming after a meal like this because you will sink like a stone.

The hotel and Therme offer a number of packages ranging from a four-night stressbuster at half-board to 13 nights at full board for a slimming cure, with the added incentive of a one percent discount for every pound lost. You usually have one spa treatment a day, although time spent in the baths is unlimited. For the rest of the day there are miles of mountain tracks to follow or, in the winter, there is skiing up the valley.

THERME VALS
CH-7132 VALS
SWITZERLAND
TEL: +41 81 926 8080
FAX: +41 81 926 8000
WWW.THERME-VALS.CH

Ulpotha, Ulpotha Village, Sri Lanka

The Ulpotha is the antithesis of traditional concepts of luxury living. It has no electric light, no hot running water and no en suite bathrooms. The bedrooms do not have walls and guests need to bring their own towels. And yet it is one of the most exclusive and serene rejuvenation retreats that you will ever be lucky enough to visit.

ABOVE: THE RECEPTION

In so many cases the term "ecotourism" seems a contradiction in terms: how can groups of strangers visit a place without spoiling some part of it? However, Ulpotha, a rural village three hours from the Sri Lankan capital Colombo, proves that it can be done. Once the center of a thriving farming community, the village slowly disintegrated to ruins after its water system fell into disrepair in the 1960s.

In 1994 three friends embarked on a venture to transform Ulpotha from its status as a decomposing wreck into an organic farming village employing traditional agricultural methods. The project has been an outstanding success, and to finance its continued restoration and ongoing

maintenance Ulpotha opens its doors to a small number of paying visitors for about four months of the year. By putting a cap on the number of guests, the village protects itself from environmental damage.

As soon as you arrive at Ulpotha, you realize why it is known as a sanctuary — hidden in the jungle, it feels like entering a time warp. Wattle-and-daub thatched buildings are hidden below scented trees; some with apricot-colored walls stained with a dye made by soaking flower petals in water. There is no noise from machinery, just the tweets, chirrups and squeaks of the surrounding wildlife. It is the perfect backdrop for kicking off your worries, along with your shoes.

LEFT: THE RESERVOIR WHERE GUESTS TAKE A DAILY SWIM

ABOVE: AN OPEN-AIR BEDROOM

ABOVE: A MEDITATION CLASS

The pace of life at Ulpotha is very slow and the mood very laid back. There is no strict timetable governing what everyone does or when they do it. If you want a treatment you just ask for it and, if the appropriate person is around, you will have it there and then. If not, you can fill in the time by relaxing and reading a book in the ambalama — the cushion-strewn pavilion — or wander down to swim in the lake with its mass of colorful lotus flowers.

Some of the steam treatments available in the wedegedera — the native healing center — are so old that they predate Ayurveda, the Indian form of naturopathy. Lying on a mat, suspended over pots of boiling water and herbal infusions, you steam like a Christmas pudding until you have released the requisite amount of toxins into the sandalwood paste that covers you from head to toe. Next, you sit on a small wooden stool to be washed with warm water infused with leafy herbs. The aged medicine man who presides over the wedegedera grinds up herbs in front of you to make pastes that cure everything from headaches and coughs to jet lag.

Massage is always available, although it is difficult to predict what type it will be since it depends entirely on who is staying at the time. Ulpotha attracts some of the world's best therapists, who visit while on sabbatical to enjoy the surroundings as much as the guests do. It does not matter if you are unfamiliar with a certain therapy: you can rest assured that whatever is on offer will be of the highest standard. In the past, treatments have included reiki, inversion therapy, zero balancing and Swedish massage.

The majority of visitors travel to Ulpotha to practise yoga because the village is a magnet for world-famous teachers. You can spend up to four or five hours a day in small, intimate classes studying all forms of the discipline from ashtanga and hatha through contact and iyengar. The classes, which are suitable for all levels and are completely optional, take place on a purpose-built shaded platform surrounded by tropical fruit trees and butterflies the size of your hand that shimmer in the bushes. Every now and again some of the village's water buffalo are herded past — it is quite a novel experience to watch them while standing on your head.

Ulpotha is completely self-sustaining and all the food served is grown organically on the farm. Meals are eaten off large palm leaves while sitting on multicolored cushions in the ambalama. The food is vegetarian and features delicate curries and a huge array of exotic dishes – steamed cassava, okra with ginger, beetroot with star anise, breadfruit and wholegrain chapattis. Along with the salads and buffalo curds, there is fruit picked fresh from the trees including miniature bananas, papaya and mango. The staple accompaniment is Ulpotha's unique strain of red rice, which not only feeds the village, but is also exported to health-food shops worldwide.

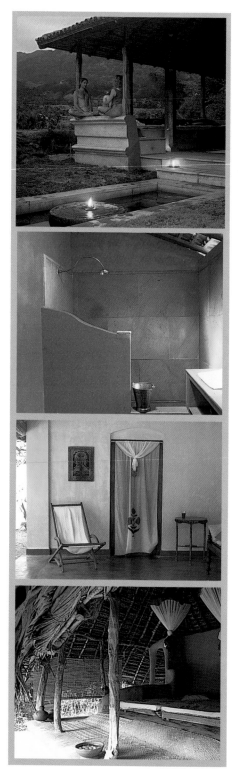

Alcohol is not banned, but neither is it served. Instead, most guests stick to fresh fruit juices, herbal infusions or water drawn straight from the bubbling spring. The latter is completely pure and safe to drink.

Because of the lack of electricity, the rhythms of the day tend to coincide with the hours of light and darkness, so it is early to bed and early to rise. Although the sandy paths to the sleeping huts are illuminated by oil lamps and glow worms, it is a good idea to pack a flashlight. The jungle suddenly seems very close, but there is no cause to feel afraid – a villager will keep an eye on your hut throughout the night to make sure you have no unpleasant surprises. The beautifully designed thatched huts have extremely comfortable beds with mosquito nets, and are furnished with traditional village textiles and earthenware, including bowls of scented temple flowers floating on water.

You will end up bathing in the mountain lake at least once a day and it is invigorating to immerse yourself under one of the waterfalls for an ad hoc massage. Guests can borrow wobbly old bicycles and find new lakes to swim in or visit one of the other villages close by. The miles and miles of mountain tracks feature spectacular scenery and a wealth of bird life including egrets, cranes and flocks of parakeets.

This part of Sri Lanka has been inhabited for thousands of years and there are many ancient ruins and temples to explore. Informal excursions are organized from Ulpotha depending on what everyone feels like doing.

By the end of your two-week stay the only thing you will regret is having to return to the real world. But when you do, you will feel more relaxed and pampered than if you had spent your entire holiday knee-deep in fluffy towels at a five-star hotel.

ABOVE: OFFERINGS ARE PLACED UNDER A PAINTING OF BUDDHA IN THE MAIN HOUSE

ULPOTHA
C/O NEAL'S YARD AGENCY
BCM NEAL'S YARD
LONDON WC1N 3XX
TEL/FAX: +44 (0)870 444 2702
INFO@ULPOTHA.COM
WWW.ULPOTHA.COM

Here is the ultimate destination spa — 900 meters (3,000 feet) above the River Ganges lies the Ananda in the Himalayas. The journey to reach it is not for the faint-hearted: a long-haul flight to Delhi, followed by a four-hour train trip and then an hour's drive up a spiraling corkscrew of a road. But when you finally arrive, the Ananda — which means bliss and contentment in Sanskrit — more than lives up to its name.

Wellness Center at the Ananda, India

Run by the Mandarin Oriental Hotel Group, the Ananda is both exotic and luxurious. With its 30 acres of hillside, the retreat is almost the size of a small village. Set in the opulent grounds of a maharaja's palace, it provides a holistic approach to the rejuvenation of mind, body and soul through both Western and Eastern therapies. Many other spas around the world offer this mix, so you may wonder why you should submit yourself to such an assault course of a journey just to reach this one.

The answer is simple. The Ananda is situated in an area famed for its spiritual teachings – the sacred city of Rishikesh, cradled in the valley below, is the birthplace of yoga and meditation; virtually all the therapists have trained in Kerala, the birthplace of Ayurveda. As a result, everything experienced at the Ananda – the sights, smells, sounds and treatments – is probably closer to what was being practiced 5,000 years ago than anything else in the world today. This is the authentic home of spiritual and physical healing, and with the emphasis on health rather than beauty it appeals to both sexes equally.

ABOVE: A SHIRODHARA TREATMENT

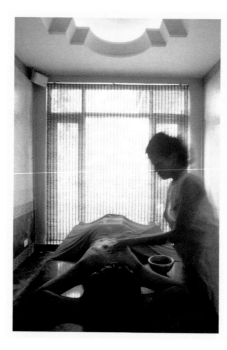

ABOVE: HERBAL POWDERS ARE USED IN A
UDWARTHANAM MASSAGE

ABOVE: THE SCENTED JACUZZI

Although each stay begins with a consultation with both Western- and Eastern-trained doctors, the focus at the Ananda is on Ayurvedic medicine. This ancient Indian therapy is based on the principle that well-being comes from the balance between three vital energies in the body, known as doshas. Working in tandem, the physicians will determine your dosha type and will then provide a diet sheet advising on the most beneficial foods for your system, as well a specialized program of massage, exercise and purification treatments. If you want to achieve spiritual enlightenment combined with a substantial loss of cellulite, they will do their very best to ensure that both happen.

Describing the Ayurvedic treatments cannot ever do them justice. The udwarthanam is a synchronized massage involving a rub with dry herbal powders, and is immensely soothing. For abhyanga, two masseurs massage medicated herbal oil into the shoulders, chest, neck and back to improve eyesight, detoxify the system and improve sleep.

Most mystical of all are the shirodhara and thakradhara therapies. With the former a stream of medicated oil is poured on to the center of the forehead for half an hour. This is said to calm the mind, improve memory and ward off senile dementia. It is very powerful, and for those staying for only a few nights the doctors usually recommend the milder thakradhara, in which buttermilk is used in place of oil. The sour smell is mildly off-putting, but even if the experience does not mesmerize you straight to sleep, you will certainly be left with a trancelike feeling of stillness for several hours afterward.

Other, more mainstream massage variations
to experience include Thai, Swedish,
shiatsu, aromatherapy, hydrotherapy and
reflexology, as well as a full range of
beauty therapies using Aveda products.
The Ananda has its own specially developed
aromatic oils, which are used in many of
the treatments. The ingredients of the oils
change with the seasons and their light
fragrances spread throughout the retreat.

The treatments available may be many
thousands of years old, but the spa center
itself is packed with state-of-the-art
equipment including a gym, sauna, squash
court, steam rooms, pebbled pools that
massage your feet and 13 treatment rooms.

After you have arrived at the Ananda and checked in at the restored nineteenth-century viceroy's palace at the center of the resort, a golf buggy will sweep you off to one of the 75 bedrooms situated in a simple, purpose-built block. Architecturally this building may be something of a let-down after the extravagance of the reception area, but once you enter your room all is forgiven — each one is stylish and airy, and the wide-angled view straight down into the Ganges valley gives the surreal feeling of being outdoors while inside. Each room also has a balcony, usually spacious enough for a spot of private yoga. The usual modern conveniences include 24-hour room service and satellite television, but spending time watching MTV in these surroundings seems criminal.

Each morning starts with a cup of fresh lemon, honey and ginger tea followed by a sunrise meditation at about 6:30 A.M. and then yoga in the music pavilion. There may be time for a quick treatment before breakfast, which normally consists of fruit, nuts, cereals and omelettes. The food at the Ananda is prepared according to the principles of Ayurveda so only the freshest herbs, spices, meats and vegetables are used in the mild curries and other delicious dishes. European meals are served, too, with low-calorie variations.

A good pair of walking shoes is important for a stay at the Ananda. Exploring the local area is encouraged and there are exhilarating hikes into the Himalayas, the Rajaji National Park, the Corbett National Park and the Chilla Sanctuary, with the opportunity to see a wide variety of wild life including almost 300 species of birds. A trip down to Rishikesh in time for evening prayers is essential — the sight of thousands of votive candles and oil lamps floating down the river is magical.

One of the joys of the Ananda is that you do not have to think at all if you would rather not. If you follow one of the dosha programs, your activities, food and treatments are all planned for you. For an adult the total freedom from having to make a single decision is extraordinarily refreshing, and ensures that the experience is a retreat in the fullest sense.

ABOVE: EVENING PRAYERS AT RISHIKESH

THE PALACE ESTATE, NARENDRA NAGAR
TEHRI – GARHWAL, UTTARANCHAL – 249175
TEL: +91 1378 27500
FAX: +91 1378 27550
ADMINISTRATOR@ANANDASPA.COM
WWW.ANANDASPA.COM

As we grow older it can become increasingly difficult to stay fit. A sedentary lifestyle combined with too much junk food can lead to feelings of lethargy, and muscles and tendons grow weaker and are more prone to injury. The boundless energy of childhood seems light-years away.

RIGHT: SWIMMING UP HIDDEN SEA CREEKS

Wild Fitness
Watamu, Kenya

ABOVE: THE MOORISH ARCH LEADING TO BARAKA HOUSE

Wild Fitness aims to help you regain the vitality of youth — irrespective of age. The spa focuses on helping its guests achieve "primal" fitness, such as our ancestors had in order to survive in the wild. Highly trained instructors use the most up-to-date techniques and equipment to help visitors improve their agility, strength, balance and stamina. But it is not a survival training course — this is fitness that is fun.

Here guests stay in Baraka House, a private coral-built residence that overlooks one of the top ten beaches in the world, cocooned from the worries of everyday life. The natural environment — sand, dunes, sea and forest — becomes an endlessly variable playground. Adventure is key and no two days at Wild Fitness are the same, whether you are floating on your back down hidden jungle creeks or running through the ancient Arabuko Sokoke Forest where elephant shrews scuttle in the bushes beside you.

All fitness levels are catered to, from supreme athletes to couch potatoes, and special exercises are developed for anyone coping with injuries. The list of activities is impressive, but there is no pressure to perform; you can train as hard as you like or take a more gentle approach, depending on how you feel. Moreover, relaxation is an important part of the spa's philosophy. Evenings often end with guests sitting quietly on the roof, contemplating the Milky Way, with a drink in one hand and a fresh oyster in the other.

The spa is situated in a strip of forest overlooking the Indian Ocean and the beauty of the surrounding area means that even the hardest training is never a chore. Strenuous activities, such as beachside circuit training and rooftop boxercise, are usually performed in the morning and early evening when the heat is less intense. When the sun is at its highest there are peaceful pursuits, such as yoga and meditation in the thatched, open-walled dhojo where monkeys play in the trees above.

The instructors are remarkably inspiring and even seem to make skipping relatively entertaining. Invariably guests achieve more than they ever imagined possible, whether completing a four-kilometer (four-mile) swim down the staggeringly beautiful Mida Creek or enjoying a twilight run in a swamp.

For those who enjoy watersports there are few better places to indulge their passion. Baraka House, where the courses are run, overlooks a coral reef that is ideal for diving and is home to some of the most spectacular marine life in the world. The area is also famous for deep-sea fishing and was one of Ernest Hemingway's favorite hunting grounds. Trips to catch marlin and tuna are easily arranged. Those of a less adventurous nature can enjoy limitless snorkeling and windsurfing.

Squash and tennis are also available at Ocean Sports, a colonial-style hotel that is just a gentle 20-minute walk along the beach from Baraka House.

Mental relaxation is an integral part of the healing process at Wild Fitness. Baraka House sleeps a maximum of eight people at a time so there is none of the disturbance typical of larger resorts where guests are continually coming and going. The house has panoramic views over the forest and the ocean, and – although close to the village of Watamu – feels pleasantly isolated. There are no televisions, radios or newspapers, and the only sounds come from the sea lapping on the shore, the birds and the small troupes of monkeys that live in the surrounding trees. It is an amazingly peaceful and safe environment, where the anxieties of the outside world completely disappear.

This feeling of well-being is augmented by 90-minute aromatherapy massages and reflexology sessions. These take place on the first floor of a thatched house set back in the forest. There are no walls to the building, only waist-high woven parapets that allow an uninterrupted view of the surrounding foliage while the balmy breeze wafts in from the sea.

ABOVE: BARBECUES ON THE BEACH

ABOVE: PERFECTING MUSCLE TONE AND BALANCE

ABOVE: LEARNING TO KITE-SURF

Wild Fitness, Watamu, Kenya   151

The food at Wild Fitness is simple and plentiful. It has to be — because of the amount of exercise, appetites are enormous. The diet includes lots of locally grown fruit, and fish is served regularly, fresh from the ocean. A professional nutritionist attends each course and gives lectures explaining how the body metabolizes different food groups and how its needs change as activity levels increase. The importance of good hydration is particularly stressed. Like the exercise programs, the course encourages guests — through example and education — to maintain a healthy regime once they return home.

LEFT: BARAKA HOUSE

ABOVE: CANOEING IN MIDA CREEK

Wild Fitness runs courses throughout the year. The weather is usually warm and dry, the hottest months being December, January and February. But however high the temperature rises, Baraka House is always cooled by sea breezes. Watamu is a malarial area so it is advisable to take appropriate medication and precautions before and during your stay.

This spa is impossibly romantic and certainly not a place to bring children. Because there are so few distractions there is time to appreciate the people around you and the opportunity to share magical experiences like watching turtles hatch in the moonlight or walking for miles along totally empty beaches.

WILD FITNESS
C/O INDIGO
SUITE 36 VICARAGE HOUSE
58–60 KENSINGTON CHURCH STREET
LONDON W8 4DB UK
TEL: +44 7937 4325
FAX: +44 7937 3400
TARAWOOD@WILDFITNESS.COM
WWW.WILDFITNESS.COM

"To-hell-u-ride!" was the cry that accompanied young men in search of fortune as they boarded the trains destined for the Colorado gold mines. Nowadays the town that most of them arrived at — Telluride — is as far from hell as you can imagine. Surrounded by the massive peaks of the San Juan Mountains, it is one of the country's foremost winter sports areas with more than 1,700 acres of snow-covered slopes for skiing and snowboarding. In summer and autumn, the staggering natural beauty of the open plains, jagged crags and golden forests is a magnet for climbers, trekkers and other adventurers.

Wyndham Peaks Resort, Telluride, Colorado

ABOVE: THE WYNDHAM PEAKS RESORT IN
THE SAN JUAN MOUNTAINS

A ten-minute drive away, at an altitude of 2,850 meters (9,500 feet) lies the Wyndham Peaks Resort, one of the country's most popular destination retreats. An imposing building, it has a somewhat harsh exterior that disguises a luxurious interior where floor-to-ceiling windows look directly out over the mountains. In the winter you can ski straight to the slopes and on sunny days, if you decide to relax on one of the vast sun-loungers, you can hear the whoosh of skiers zipping past on nearby trails. Dive from snow-covered steps into a steaming heated outdoor pool or watch as other guests whizz down toward you via the interconnecting waterslide from the indoor lap pool above.

Not only does Wyndham Peaks have the advantage of being set in the most magnificent location, it is also home to the Golden Door Spa, 3,700 square meters (42,000 square feet) dedicated purely to healing, fitness and beauty. The spa draws its inspiration from the ancient honjin inns of Japan, where exhausted travelers would stop to recharge their batteries, and its 44 treatment rooms, with their awe-inspiring views, are serenely minimalist.

The emphasis at the Golden Door Spa is on purification. It combines a variety of techniques from around the world, including Oriental massage and aromatherapy, Ayurvedic treatments, hydrotherapy and even healing rituals used by the Southern Utes, the Native American tribe who once populated the San Juan Mountains.

Before any treatments, guests are taken to the Kivas (the Native American term for locker room) for the Peaks Purification Ritual. Here you are greeted with a fluffy robe, towel, slippers and a cup of detoxifying herbal tea. Next, you are invited to relax and breathe in the revitalizing scents of eucalyptus and juniper in the steam room. If the steam begins to make your eyes sting there are bowls of chilled cucumber and iced facecloths on hand to cool your face before moving on to the sauna. The ritual's final stage is a dip in the mineral-enriched whirlpool where you wallow quietly and watch the activity on the slopes through giant picture windows.

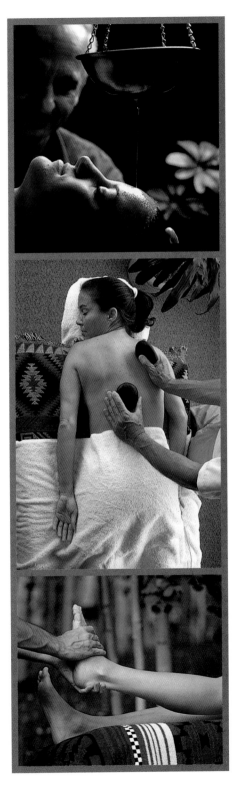

The mountain air around the resort is pure and invigorating, but the altitude is enough to make some people feel slightly ill with headaches, insomnia and nausea. To combat this the spa has a Breathe Easy program providing an oxygen facial or body exfoliation, which, apart from any other benefits, are said to lead to healthier, younger-looking skin. At the O2 Bar you can relax in a vibrating chair and breathe in concentrated oxygen for up to an hour, which leaves you feeling bouncy and incredibly clearheaded. The treatment is also an extremely effective hangover cure.

Given the nature of its surroundings, fitness features high on the spa's menu of things to do. Classes include spinning, Step, Pilates, yoga and meditation. The gym boasts a Cybex weight room, a cardiovascular deck, squash and racquetball courts, and three indoor rock-climbing walls; there are instructors on hand to help you in all these activities. From a scientific point of view, Body Composition Analysis, Cardio Coaching and Nutritional Analysis are all available.

Although guests under the age of sixteen are not allowed to visit the spa, a special KidSpa combines excitement, education and entertainment for children from six months to eleven years old. Teenagers have a choice of a Teen Facial, Thai Massage, supervised climbing sessions and prospecting for gold in nearby streams.

ABOVE: THE PEAKS RESORT AND SPA

Whatever the time of year, the Wyndham Peaks Resort provides the perfect playground for excitement seekers. Some of the ski trails cover almost vertical descents of 1,050 meters (3,500 feet). You can charter a helicopter to drop you off on untracked powder runs or go cross-country skiing for miles and miles through the undulating forests. Ski valets at the hotel will helpfully warm your boots and tune your skis overnight and, if you are not skiing or snowboarding, you can opt to go snowmobiling or dog-sledding instead.

When the snow melts, the Rocky Mountains become the location for even more activities. The hiking is spectacular and you can follow the age-old trails created by the Ute Indian fur traders and then latterly by the goldminers. To reach the rather eerie abandoned mining towns of Tomboy, Alta and Smugglers Union, it is best to go by Jeep. All that now remains of the settlements where the prospectors once lived are teetering skeletal buildings clinging precariously to the mountainside.

WYNDHAM PEAKS RESORT & GOLDEN DOOR SPA
136 COUNTRY CLUB DRIVE
P.O. BOX 2702
TELLURIDE MOUNTAIN VILLAGE CO 81435
TEL: +1 970 728 6800
FAX: +1 970 728 6175
EMAIL: DCAREY@WYNDHAM.COM
WWW.THEPEAKSRESORT.COM

Experienced mountaineers can tackle the nearby peaks of Mount Wilson and El Diente, which rate as two of the most difficult climbs in the area. White-water rafting, fly fishing, tennis, horseback riding and golf at the 18-hole championship course (which encircles the Wyndham Peaks) are other favored alternatives. Telluride itself is fascinating. Once the setting for Butch Cassidy's first bank robbery (in 1889 when he escaped with $20,000), it now plays host to a number of acclaimed annual cultural events including festivals for wine, jazz, bluegrass, chamber music and film.

In keeping with the rugged backdrop, the decor in the Wyndham Peaks leans toward a marriage of chic with Native American. Colossal windows feature everywhere, while leather and suede furniture mixes with giant hearths, stone-flagged floors and brightly woven throws and rugs. The 174 bedrooms, 27 penthouses and 11 cabins are elegantly rustic, with the cabins in particular suitable for family groups.

Food is served in the two restaurants — the Appaloosa and Legends — and concentrates on fresh seasonal ingredients such as elk medallions from the high country, seared trout from local lakes and peaches from Colorado's lower-altitude orchards. Despite the healthy options (which shun oil, butter and cream) and the large amount of exercise, it can be tricky losing weight. The temptations are great, the portions are enormous and the choice bewildering — at breakfast alone there are up to six different types of milk from which to choose.

The publisher would like to thank the following photographers, agencies and organizations for their kind permission to reproduce the photographs in this book:

4 Paul Quayle/Axiom Photographic Agency; 6 left and right Daintree Ecolodge & Spa; 6 center Chris Caldicott/Axiom Photographic Agency; 7 left Nicholas Kane/Arcaid (Architect: Peter Zumthor); 7 right Chiva Som; center Wild Fitness; 8 left Chiva Som; 8 right and center Ananda in the Himalayas; 9 right John Miles/Panos Pictures; 9 center Wyndham Peaks Resort; 10 above left Giles Caldicott/Axiom Photographic Agency; 10 below left and 11 Todd Eberle courtesy of Ian Shrager Hotels; 12 Jenny Acheson/Axiom Photographic Agency; 13 Todd Eberle courtesy of Ian Shrager Hotels; 14 Jenny Acheson/Axiom Photographic Agency; 15 left James Davis Worldwide; 15 right Todd Eberle courtesy of Ian Shrager Hotels; 16 Georgia Glynn-Smith courtesy of Babington House; 17 left Edina Van Der Wyck/The Interior Archive (property: Babington House); 18 above Georgia Glynn-Smith courtesy of Babington House; 18 center Edina Van Der Wyck/The Interior Archive (property: Babington House); 18 below and 19 Georgia Glynn-Smith courtesy of Babington House; 20 Adam Woolfitt/Corbis; 21 left Edina Van der Wyck/The Interior Archive (property: Babington House); 21 right Georgia Glynn-Smith courtesy of Babington House; 22–23 Ian Yates/Eye Ubiquitous; 24 James Davis Worldwide; 25 above Blue Lagoon ; 25 center Chris Caldicott/Axiom Photographic Agency; 25 below Blue Lagoon; 26 Chris Caldicott/Axiom Photographic Agency; 27 above Piers Cavendish/IMPACT; 27 below James Harris/Axiom Photographic Agency; 28 below Canyon Ranch; 28–29 Jochen Tack; 30 above left Canyon Ranch; 30 above center Jochen Tack; 30 above right–32 Canyon Ranch; 33 main picture Jochen Tack; 33 above left Canyon Ranch; 33 below left Jochen Tack; 34–39 Chiva

Som; 40 David Jacobs/Getty Images; 41–45 Jochen Tack; 46 Daintree Ecolodge & Spa; 47 James Davis Worldwide; 48–51 Daintree Ecolodge & Spa; 52–55 The Delphi Mountain Resort & Spa; 56 above left Stephen Rafferty/Eye Ubiquitous; 56 above right Bennett Dean/Eye Ubiquitous; 57 The Delphi Mountain Resort & Spa; 58 left G. Hellier/Robert Harding; 58 right Danubius Hotels Group; 59 C Martin/Axiom Photographic Agency; 60 above left David Foreman/Eye Ubiquitous; 60 above right Oscar Okapi/Camera Press; 60 below left Danubius Hotels Group; 61 C. Martin/Axiom Photographic Agency; 62 Danubius Hotels Group; 63 above left Paul Quayle/Axiom Photographic Agency; 63 above right Danubius Hotels Group; 64 Tim Clinch; 65 Tops Socquet/La Compagne des Hotels de Montagne; 66 Hans Zeegers/Taverne Agency (Styling: Marita Janssen); 67 left Tim Clinch; 67 center Bertrand Limbour/La Compagne des Hotels de Montagne; 67 right Gilles de Chabaneix/La Compagne des Hotels de Montagne; 68 left Tim Clinch; 68 right Gilles de Chabaneix/La Compagne des Hotels de Montagne; 69 Erica Lennard/La Compagne des Hotels de Montagne; 70–71 Gavin Hellier/Robert Harding; 71 below Andrew Wood/The Interior Archive; 72 Courtesy of The Legian, Bali; 73 Hans Zeegers/Taverne Agency (Styling: Marita Janssen); 74 above Andrew Wood/The Interior Archive; 74 Courtesy of The Legian, Bali; 75 main picture Andrew Wood/The Interior Archive; 75 above left Courtesy of The Legian, Bali; 75 below left Hans Zeegers/Taverne Agency (Styling: Marita Janssen); 76–77 Jochen Tack; 78 above John Miles/Panos Pictures; 78 below Jochen Tack; 79 Getty Images/Sylvain Grandadam; 80–81 Jochen Tack; 82–84 Mikkel Vang/Vogue Entertaining; 85 The Mansion Hotel Group (Earl Carter courtesy of The Mansion House Hotel); 86 above left Gavin Helllier/Robert Harding; 86 above center The Mansion Hotel Group (Earl Carter courtesy of Mansion House Hotel); 86 above right Mikkel Vang/

Vogue Entertaining; 87 The Mansion Hotel Group (Earl Carter courtesy of Mansion House Hotel); 88 ZFL PR (A. Lampelmayr courtesy of Mayr Health Spa); 89 Adam Woolfitt/Robert Harding; 90–93 A. Lampelmayr courtesy of Mayr Health Spa; 94–99 above left Chris Caldicott; 99 above right W.Louvet/VISA/CEDRI/IMPACT; 99 below right Chris Caldicott; 100 Santuary Zara Spa; 101 above Christopher Rennie/Robert Harding; 101 below Sanctuary Zara Sap; 102 left Mark Henley/IMPACT; 102 right–105 Sanctuary Zara Spa; 106–107 Tim Hall/Axiom Photographic Agency; 107 below–110 above center Les Sources de Caudalie; 110 above right Paul Raftery; 111 Les Sources de Caudalie; 112–113 Pangkor Laut; 114 left Tim Page/Eye Ubiquitous; 114 right–117 Pangkor Laut; 118–123 Starwood Hotels & Resorts Worldwide Inc; 124 below Forte Village Resort; 124–125 Ellen Rooney/Axiom Photographic Agency; 126–128 above left and above right Ann Scott Associates (Forte Village Resort); 128 below Robert Harding; 129 Ann Scott Associates; 130–131 Nicholas Kane/Arcaid (Architect: Peter Zumthor); 132 Paul Almasy/Corbis; 133–134 Nicholas Kane/Arcaid (Architect: Peter Zumthor); 135 below H.P. Schutlz courtesy of Therme Vals (Architect: Peter Zumthor); 136 Chris Simpson courtesy of Ulpotha; 137–138 left Simon Upton/The Interior Archive; 138 right Courtesy of Ulpotha; 139 Simon Upton/The Interior Archive; 140 above Courtesy of Ulpotha; 140–141 Simon Upton/The Interior Archive; 142–147 Ananda in the Himalayas; 148–153 Indigo PR(Wild Fitness); 154–155 Wyndham Peaks Resort; 156 D. Jacobs/Robert Harding; 157–159 Wyndham Peaks Resort

Every effort has been made to trace the copyright holders for photographs. We apologize in advance for any unintentional omission and would be pleased to insert the appropriate acknowledgment in any subsequent editions.